Thailand
CONFIDENTIAL

Jerry Hopkins

D0097326

PERIPLUS

Published by Periplus Editions (HK) Ltd, with editorial offices at
130 Joo Seng Road #06-01/03, Singapore 368357.

ISBN 0-7946-0093-X

Printed in Singapore

Distributed by:

North America, Latin America & Europe
Tuttle Publishing
364 Innovation Drive
North Clarendon, VT 05759-9436
Tel: (802) 773 8930; Fax: (802) 773 6993
Email: info@tuttlepublishing.com
www.tuttlepublishing.com

Japan
Tuttle Publishing
Yaekari Building 3F,
5-4-12 Osaki, Shinagawa-ku,
Tokyo 141-0032
Tel: (03) 5437 0171; Fax: (03) 5437 0755
Email: tuttle-sales@gol.com

Asia Pacific
Berkeley Books Pte Ltd
130 Joo Seng Road #06-01/03, Singapore 368357
Tel: (65) 6280 1330; Fax: (65) 6280 6290
Email: inquiries@periplus.com.sg
www.periplus.com

09 08 07 06 05
5 4 3 2 1

A grumpy expat sounds off on other expats and foreigners, penis worship, tourists, Bangkok's bodysnatchers, piracy, back-packers, aphrodisiacs, fast elephants, dangerous elephants, rotten fish, a gay water buffalo, ghosts, scams and cons, shadow wives, sex-change operations and ladyboys, country music, fear and respect, drugs, the beer wars, bi-racial cool, street food, superlatives, denial, eating insects, violence, making movies, Thai time, learning the language, chili peppers, a heart attack, the rubber barons, the King's music, Thai whisky, sex, and other amazing stuff you'll never read about in any guide to Thailand.

"Hopkin's is just the man to capture the magical, impossible carnival that is Thailand, his expat's perspective putting the country's traditions, customs and quirks in high relief. The author clearly has a voracious and adventurous appetite, and Thailand provides the perfect feast. He devours subjects ranging from the sex trade and local cuisine to magic tattoos and the kingdom's 'swinging monarch'. After over a decade in the country, Hopkins knows and loves his subject dearly–that much is obvious–and his vivid portrait projects that love from every page."

— *Jann Wenner*

"A loving exposé of everything that's wonderful about Thailand, and much that isn't. Should be required reading for all new comers".

— *Joe Cummings*

"Wanna stand in the face of a charging elephant, get hit by a motorcycle, eat giant water bugs, blowtorch your mouth on some of the hottest chili peppers on earth, then go watch a sex change operation? Of course you don't, but, happily, Jerry Hopkins has done all that and more—lots more—in this darkly humorous, deeply affectionat, clear eyed but never patronizing portrait of Thailand, his adopted home. Highly recommended."

— *Tim Cahill, author of Lost in My Own Backyard,*
Hold the Enlightenment, and Jaguars Ripped My Flesh

Contents

Confessions of a Grumpy Old Expat

When people asked me why I chose to leave Hawaii—nearly everyone's idea of paradise—and moved to Thailand, I had an answer so long it qualified as a speech. I started visiting Thailand sometime in the 1980s, I said—so often it sounded as if I were pulling a string in one of those Chatty Cathy doll's necks, giving a recorded reply—and by 1993, I was spending as much time in Southeast Asia as in the United States. I had lived too long in the islands, where every day was precisely like the last and I knew the next would be the same. I was single, my kids from a long dissolved marriage were grown and gone, and I figured I had enough money put aside to last two years, so I decided to go where it seemed more interesting.

I picked Thailand over other countries—I droned on—for its hospitable population, alluring women, light-yet-healthy cuisine, affordable cost of living, historic culture and varied geography, tropical climate, the most interesting expat community I'd encountered anywhere, the contemplative nature of Buddhism (and its lack of a god or dogmatic creed), a reasonably free press, an entertaining government and an abiding sense of fun. It also had a major city where there was cable TV and the phones worked most of the time, whose location was proximate to just about everywhere else I wanted to spend most of the rest of my life; in under three hours I could be anywhere from Hong Kong to Bali to Kathmandu. There was a rawness, a messiness, an attitude that defied Western-style logic. Thailand was a place where time wasn't linear, and property was given more value than life.

Like most new arrivals to Thailand, after I'd been here for six months, I thought I knew everything there was to know. At the two-year mark, I was beginning to have some doubts, and now, after more than ten years, I realize I'll probably never understand a damned thing about the place and its residents. That doesn't mean I don't sometimes pretend to know, and about a third of the little "essays" and stories in this book illustrate this delusion.

I am, by training, a journalist, and by nature what might fairly be called a grumpy old man. As a journalist, I'm from the old school. I'm not one of those gonzo types who never let a fact get in the way of a good story. At the same time, I recognize that there is no such thing as objectivity, only degrees of subjectivity, and even the best of us tend to present the facts according to circumstance, mood, biography and biases. I'm male, white, sixty-something, American, well educated, a social liberal raised as a Quaker, a family man, a cynic with a twisted sense of humor and an expat living in a foreign country totally unlike the one I came from, where I now have a big Thai family and spend a lot of time with poor people, in the slums of Bangkok as well as in the rural countryside. All that, and a lot more, comes into play, no matter what I do, think, and write.

In all the time I've lived in Thailand, I've only written one letter to the editor, and that was to ask that the numerous and mysterious Thai holidays be announced in the newspapers the day before so that dummies like me will know when banks, the post office and government offices are going to be closed. My suggestion was ignored. I don't expect any action to follow any of my opinions stated here, either.

It will be clear to the reader which of the forty-two "chapters" are rants, and I say in my defense only that this is what expats probably do best. I'm a member of a loose group of expatriated malcontents called "chairs." We meet every Saturday for coffee and complaints. It gives us an opportunity to feel superior. We have all the answers and solutions—just ask us. Make me prime minister and I'll fix everything!

The truth is, we wouldn't have it any other way. Because living in Thailand is never less than fascinating, beneath all the grime still exotic and always a surprise.

Thailand is easy to criticize. What country isn't? (Don't ask me about the United States, unless you're prepared to get sprayed with saliva and vitriol.) I have a file labeled "Thai Troubles." In it are newspaper articles and various official reports saying that out of twenty-one million children, one in five suffers from physical or mental abuse...that thanks to all the artesian wells tapping its ground water and the dumping of so much steel and cement on top in uncontrolled development, Bangkok sinks twelve centimeters (four and a half inches) a year, so that much of the city already is below sea level...that one of every three billboards is illegal and unsafe...that AIDS is the leading cause of death nationwide and life expectancy for the average Thai is falling...that there are up to three thousand high-rise buildings in Bangkok that pose "grave risk" of collapse (the government refuses to name them; rumor has it that several house movie theaters)...that more than half the vehicles on the road in the capital exceed the legal exhaust fume level...that only 104 of the two thousand fresh food markets in the country meet hygiene standards set by the Public Health Ministry and ninety percent of the meat sold in markets comes from dirty and unsanitary slaughterhouses... that every day more than a million cubic meters of untreated waste water is released into the Chao Phrya River...that more than four hundred species of wildlife are on the brink of extinction...that since 1932, when the absolute monarchy was replaced by a constitutional monarchy, the nation has had twenty-nine governments, twenty coups d'etat and seventeen constitutions...and that according to the Health Department, more than half of all public toilets in Thailand are unhygienic, smelly, dirty and damp.

That's not all. Little seems to make any sense here. Even the most critical activists admit that Thailand has some of the best environmental laws in the world, but they, like most rules governing behavior are ignored or bent. Motorcyclists use the sidewalks as if they were lanes in the roadway and there are so many vendors and other obstructions, pedestrians frequently are forced to walk in the streets with some of the most horrendous traffic in the world. (And likely encounter an elephant!) Thailand has the highest rate of road fatalities in the world and no public ambulances. When cops and military officers are caught doing something illegal, they aren't charged and tried, they are assigned to "an inactive post." Thais don't walk, they meander, drifting all over the footpaths, looking in one direction while moving in another, bumping into people, like children seeming unaware that anyone else might be nearby. Two recent Miss Thailands were raised in the United States and unable to speak Thai fluently. Businesses spend a fortune on advertising, signage, menus, etc., where the attempts at English spelling and grammar are so mangled they are as humorous as they are sad. Order a meal in a restaurant and the cook will put the easy-to-prepare dishes on first, the longer-to-cook and more complex orders last, so that diners who came in together get served one at a time and they don't get to eat together.

That's not all. Squatters and pocket slums are commonly found in otherwise wealthy neighborhoods, roosters adding their hiccupy morning cries to the purr of Mercedes Benzes being driven to work. Time is circular rather than linear. Thais eat six, seven, eight times a day and remain thin. Women take their clothes off to dance in nightclubs, but at seaside resorts enter the water dressed from ankle to neck. (Money driving the nudity, shyness the public cover-up.) Thais won't work in an abattoir because killing violates a Buddhist law, yet they matter-of-factly murder each other. (And know precisely what to do—with gusto and imagination—when the butchered pig or steer shows up in the kitchen.) In a country of sixty-two million, the incidence of mobile phone ownership is projected to reach fifty percent by 2005, while seventy percent of the population barely ekes out a subsistence living on the land. Thus, there is an illusion of modernity, but many (some say most) of Thailand's citizens (even the rich ones) cling tenaciously to feudal codes and Stone Age belief systems.

To put it simply, Thailand in many ways is a Third World country posing as a Developing Nation or NEC (Newly Emerging Country), a runny-nosed kid in a counterfeit designer tee-shirt with his nose pressed to the window of a gold shop.

It is a place where there is a whoopsy sense of improvisation at play. Thais can fall asleep anywhere, both quickly and comfortably: piled in a heap like puppies on the floor, beneath a sidewalk stall, atop a motorcycle. Because there are so many times when shoes must be taken off—not only when entering a temple but also anyone's house—shoes are worn as if they were rubber slippers, the heels flattened rather than fitted into. Give three ingredients to a Thai cook (and men as well as women can cook) and he or she will produce half a dozen world class dishes. Take a wrist watch to one of the sidewalk vendors who serve much of Bangkok's needs for timepiece repair, and the three primary tools in use may be a broken, counterfeit Swiss army knife, eyebrow tweezers and a toothbrush.

Thailand is a place made for the phrase "Only in..." I have a friend who moved here forty years ago after reading a story about a tram car that struck a pedicab, which in turn rammed into a taxi, causing the cab to swerve and fall into a canal on top of a boat selling charcoal. "I knew then and there," he says, "that I just had to live in a place where such things happen." I read a story myself not so long ago about rat tails being burned to rid a village of sin, another about a large provincial town where some twenty five thousand people turned out to publicly curse the narcotics trade and all those involved in it, Thailand's way to "just say no." While approximately a hundred police generals were told to take a five-day meditation course to improve their efficiency, discipline and ethics. (Guns to be checked with the shoes at the door.) The same police also were banned from the nation's golf courses, an attempt—the newspapers said—to get them back to their desks. A wealthy massage parlor tycoon, who claimed he paid bribes to police amounting to millions of baht every month, ran for Governor of Bangkok in 2004 and placed a respectable third, then was asked to co-host a television talk show.

How can you not love a country where stories like this are a regular occurrence? I still believe Hawaii is the most beautiful place on earth, but in 1993, I was falling asleep under the same old palm tree every day. Hawaii may sound like Elysium to others, but to me it became a big yawn. I needed challenge again, the energy generated by surprise, the edgy feeling that accompanies disarray and portends chaos. After a lifetime of travel on five continents, I thought Bangkok was my best bet. I haven't been disappointed. The country's tourism authority had it right a couple of years ago when it called it "Amazing Thailand."

I spent several of my teenaged years reading science fiction and fantasy, living—in my head—in alien worlds, zipping back and forth in time and outer space. During the 1960s and 1970s, my lifestyle included numerous experiments with psychotropic drugs. And over the years, my friends have included circus performers, ex-cons, drug addicts, prostitutes (male and female), priests, cultists and faddists, magicians, cops and transsexuals. Today I live in Thailand. I think I'm in a rut.

Of course that is my white, male, Western, et cetera point of view. My Thai wife doesn't think Thailand is odd. When I took her to America, well, now, that country was downright weird. From her point of view. When I thought about it, I couldn't really disagree. It's just a matter of what we're used to. "I looooove *phee*," she said to me recently, when a movie about Dracula popped up on the TV screen. *Phee* is the Thai word for ghosts. I don't even believe in ghosts and she loooooves them. We're both right, of course.

So, call this book a love letter to what I think is a peculiar place. As I say later in a different context: dreams may come true in Hawaii, but in Thailand it's fantasies that come true; it even has several bars like the one in Star Wars. And if I sound as if some of what's here isn't to my exact taste or delight, I didn't like all of the drugs, either.

About a third of the material in this book was previously pub-lished in newspapers and magazines. In them, as well as in the stories written specifically for this book, I have tried to explore subjects that generally were ignored or described in travel maga-zines and guidebooks superficially, or from a fawning point of view. (I remember reading in one Big Name Guidebook that the planning in Bangkok was "haphazard," the water off Pattaya "murky.") I try here to burrow a little deeper and more honestly.

Thailand is called The Land of Smiles. I don't intend to wipe that smile off Thailand's face in the pages that follow. Only to take a look behind it. From a grumpy old *farang's* point of view.

Wild Thailand

The Ugly Truth About Elephants

You can forget all that Babar/Dumbo nonsense.

Yes, elephants are adorable and entertaining and smart and endangered and worthy of our lasting respect, but a lot of that respect should be given because many of them are among the most dangerous animals on earth, killing more people than any other mammal, save man himself. Worldwide figures are unavailable—I'll explain why soon—but it is known that in India, over two hundred are killed every year and in Thailand the toll is at least fifty. Compared to elephants, such maligned animals as snakes, crocodiles and sharks are downright friendly.

The odd thing is that the image of a man atop the largest of land mammals is a romantic one. Classic twentieth century literary and film characters, including Mowgli in Rudyard Kipling's *Jungle Book* series and Edgar Rice Burroughs's *Tarzan of the Apes* are remembered riding through the forests of Asia and Africa in loincloths, astride their pachyderm pals, forming a manly bond, forever partners and friends, nature at its most harmonious.

From childhood, we are further lulled by Disney's *Dumbo* and the Babar books and the circuses that add to the illusion of glamor and the non-threatening sense of adventure we feel when we see men with the wise and kindly modern day mammoths, teaching them to perform facile tricks.

This attitude persists in Thailand, where the annual elephant round-up in Surin, a variety of religious and royal ceremonies throughout the country, and commercial shows in Bangkok, Pattaya, Phuket and in the north from Lampang to Chiang Mai, along with the popular jungle treks, have exposed growing numbers of visitors and residents to Babar up close and personal.

In Thailand today, there are approximately twenty-three hundred elephants engaged in a variety of domestic services, mostly tourism and entertaining, and although the government legally classifies the animals as "livestock," regulating them under legislation for draught animals, according to Richard Lair, one of the world's foremost pachyderm experts, they are "wild" even if born in captivity and trained from childhood. Unlike most dogs, who evolved from wolves, the wildness hasn't been purged from elephants by selective breeding.

"Some elephants form such warm and affectionate bonds with man as to deceive the observer into thinking that this animal must have been made truly domestic," Richard wrote in a book commissioned by the United Nations and considered definitive in the field, *Gone Astray: The Care and Management of the Asian Elephant in Domesticity* (1997). "Many other elephants in domesticity, however, remain unremittingly wild, hostile to man and ready to kill him at every chance. Clearly, a domesticated elephant is simply a wild animal in chains—but a wild animal frequently gentle and intelligent enough to serve as a totally trustworthy baby-sitter to watch over human infants.

"Far quicker than its bulk would seem to allow, the elephant can kill with its tusks, its forehead, its trunk (either by striking or lifting and throwing), its mouth (by biting, a favorite of cows), its legs (by stomping or kicking), or any combination thereof. Kicks come in astonishing variety with both the front and back legs able to kick away from or into the body, the latter a perfect prelude for yet more kicking underneath the elephant's belly. A killing attack often comes as a combination of charging, kicking and head-butting so fast and so coordinated that the three components are inseparable to the eye. The domesticated elephant, thoroughly accustomed to man's presence, is particularly adept.

"In everyday management," Richard concluded, "elephants fall into three classes: some are never dangerous, some are dangerous only under very specific circumstances (in the *mahout's* absence, around trains, in water, etc.) and some are dangerous all of the time. The proportions of the classes within a group will vary somewhat according to sex-and-age structure and the quality of training, but considering every third elephant to be dangerous is a very healthy way of thinking."

The question of the day, of course, is: how do you tell the three classes of elephant apart? They don't come in different colors. This is where you have to put your faith in the people who run the zoos, circuses and Thailand's many elephant shows. Keeping in mind that everyone makes mistakes.

Richard saw his first elephants at the San Francisco Zoo as a three-year-old and claims he knew from that moment that this was, somehow, his life's work. I saw my first elephants in the Frank Buck Circus when I was in grade school, also in the United States. But where Richard's interest continued virtually uninterrupted, my first real contact with one of the brutes came when I emerged from the audience at an elephant show in Pattaya a few years ago. I'd watched other tourists lie in rows on the field in front of the bleachers, with the *mahouts*, or trainers, leading the animals over them, one careful step at a time. So I figured I was in no danger when I volunteered to have one of them wrap its trunk around my waist and lift me into the air. Once elevated and in the elephant's control, everything changed, and it was something less, or more, than a lark. A photograph taken by a friend shows an expression on my face of delight mixed with terror.

I met Richard some years later, when I was writing a story about filmmaking in Thailand. He'd worked as a consultant in the production of a movie called *Operation Dumbo Drop*, which called for an adult elephant to run down a crowded village street. Many said safety couldn't be guaranteed. After fifteen years in Thailand, Richard felt he knew the elephant he chose for the job, and under his tutelage, the elephant did the scene in one take, without causing injury to anyone or upturning a single produce cart.

Which takes us back to the third of all domesticated elephants that he feels are safest. As a tourist climbing nervously onto the back of one to go for a weaving, lumbering walk through the jungle or volunteering, as I did, to take part in an elephant show, you can only hope that the animal you meet—reaching a height of more than three meters and weighing as much as four tons—is one of them. Usually they are. Squashed and impaled tourists are bad for tourism and it happens rarely.

More often it's the keeper and the *mahout*, those who have regular contact with the beasts, who are trampled and kicked and picked up and tossed—and mostly, nowadays, it's the young *mahout*, who doesn't know what he's doing. Not so long ago, a *mahout* was respected and the craft was passed with honor from father to son. No more. In the modern world, the elephant is not needed for transportation of people and goods or for logging and *mahouts* must teach their charges tricks or, when the habitat is depleted and there is no forage, as happens every year during the dry season, take their animals to the city to beg, selling bananas and sugar cane at inflated prices to tourists or charging a small fee to Thais who believe walking under an elephant will bring good luck; not so long ago, a pregnant woman was trampled while praying her child would be male.

A *mahout's* son today would rather have the prestige and money earned driving a truck. When, instead, he's stuck taking care of a cranky, old pachyderm, and is both uninterested and ill-prepared to do so, accidents happen. Although, as Richard says, the weekly deaths in Thailand nearly always are associated with illegal logging activity, and are not reported. Thus, in Thailand, the official body count is low.

Many of these deaths are the result of the adult male coming into musth, a periodic swelling of a gland between the eye and ear that causes aggression so fierce the beast may attack humans, other elephants, and inanimate objects; from the earliest stages, they must be retired from all work assignments and chained to very large trees. If they're not, severe injury and death may come to those who aren't paying attention. (Signs to look for: grumpiness, a refusal to take a *mahout's* orders, a slight discharge from the eyes, and massive erections, although they aren't always a clue as bull elephants tend to get them year round.)

Richard and I became friends and I visited him when I could at the Thai Elephant Conservation Centre in Lampang, where he helped found what probably is the world's only *mahout* school and added elephant painting and the world's first all-elephant orchestra to the tourist show that helps raise money for the center's operations. Which also include a hospital famous for its treatment of animals who've stepped on land mines along the Thai-Burma border or have become addicted to amphetamines fed them by greedy, illegal loggers; also a refuge for nearly a hundred elephants, some of them orphaned by ivory poachers. Not long ago, I went to observe the elephant orchestra record a CD, another fundraising device.

I was standing in a grove of teak trees beside a two-ton animal that was banging on a big drum with a mallet held in his trunk. Nearby his fellow "big band" musicians were playing outsized xylophone-like instruments crafted with steel bars and a gong fashioned from an old sawmill blade. One of the *mahouts* had given another a harmonica, which all but disappeared into the end of the trunk. Not only was it difficult to take any of this seriously, all thought of danger was drowned in a rather pleasant cacophony of bonks and clangs and juicy hoots.

Richard approached me and said, "Watch it, buddy. The elephant on the drums"—only a foot or so from where I stood—"tried to kill his new assistant *mahout* yesterday."

I backed away hurriedly and asked why he was playing in the band, with so many people—including me!—in his immediate proximity.

"He's perfectly safe with his head *mahout* on his neck," Richard said, "and, besides, he's our best percussionist."

A Buffalo Named Toey

This is a story about a water buffalo named Toey, who was Nittaya Phanthachat's best friend when she was growing up on a farm in Rayong, on Thailand's eastern seaboard. Nit doesn't like cats or dogs, thinks they make poor pets. When it comes to what she calls the "buppalo," now there's another tale.

Nit was the last born of seven children, arriving seventeen years after the next youngest, one of those biological surprises that happens in any culture. By now, many of her siblings were married and having children of their own, so her closest friends growing up were not brothers and sisters, but nieces and nephews. Together, they minded the family buffaloes.

Nit talked about how her brothers labored in the fields, walking behind a wooden plow that seemed as big as they were, in partnership with the slate-black beasts ahead of them, preparing the soil for the sugar cane crop. It was Nit's job as a small child to take the animals to and from work, from the shed near the modest house where the Phanthachats lived to fields that sometimes were more than a mile away.

Nit's favorite was Toey, who had been born the same year she was, in 1952. He wasn't like the other buffalo, Nit said. His horns were curled like a mountain goat's, rather than sweeping back in a proud and characteristic scimitar-like curve. In a male buffalo, she told me, this meant he had no interest in females, thus the name given to all such animals, an abbreviation for *katoey*, the

Thai word for the transvestite, transsexual or overtly homosexual male. Toey's eyes also watered all the time, she said, as if he were crying because his horns were not like all the others in the family stable.

Nit loved Toey and sang to him while riding on his broad back, patting him on the left flank when she wanted him to turn right, on the right when she wanted him to go left. Nit also liked to whistle. She said that was the way family members found her in the fields. They listened for her whistling.

As unusual as Toey's horns were, the feeling Nit had for the animal was not. In Asia, when she was growing up, the water buffalo was not only the family tractor, but also the family friend. Because of its placid nature, it was matter-of-factly trusted as a child's "baby-sitter"; the child, of course, believed the caretaking worked the other way round.

The *bubalis bubalis*, as academics rather comically call the beast, also was, and is, given recognition on a community level, where a farmer's worth may be measured by how many buffaloes he owns. In some countries, a buffalo is still sacrificed when someone rich dies, another yardstick of wealth, and until fairly recently, before beef from cattle was imported from Australia and elsewhere, it was the region's primary source of red meat. Not so well-known is that there are herds of water buffalo stretching all the way to Italy, where the milk is made into mozzarella cheese, while in India the milk is drunk because cattle are sacred and never used for nourishment.

Buffalo in Thailand and other Southeast Asian countries additionally play a minor role in sport. In the autumn in Chon Buri, where Nit now has a home, farmers bring their strongest animals to town for the annual buffalo races. There are no saddles or reins to help the "jockeys" stay on top, little for them to hold on to but a single rope and a sandpapery back. To be judged, the buffalo and rider must arrive at the finish line simultaneously.

In Indonesia and Vietnam, water buffaloes are pitted against each other in fights. These usually take the form of slow-motion butting contests, where no animal really gets hurt. It's not at all like the National Geographic Channel series called *Born to Kill.* Maybe the buffaloes have a headache the next day, I don't know.

The bad news is that the domesticated species is dying out, as for a variety of reasons the birth rate drops and tractors replace them in the fields, sending those no longer needed to the nearest slaughterhouse. Forty years ago, there were seven million in Thailand alone, a figure now reduced by half.

This doesn't mean the species is endangered—as is the wild water buffalo, found in small numbers nowadays—but it does mean that many families no longer have them as pets or in great number. My wife Lamyai, now in her forties, remembers that when she was growing up in Isan, her father had fifty of the animals. Now the family has none.

Not long ago in Thailand, a movie maker named Aroon Pavilai used computer graphics, like those used in *Jurassic Park,* to bring a water buffalo called Mr. Buff to life, giving him the appearance of laughing, smiling, speaking, singing and crying.

Nit doesn't say Toey could do all those things, but right up to the end, he cried. Tears still ran down his cheeks, Nit told me the last time she went home to Rayong and visited him.

"Same age me," Nit said. "Porty-three! Bery old. He cannot work. He bery sad. I whistle a song to him. Remember Nit! Looking to me when I whistle."

I can see Nit and Toey in the field when they were young. Toey is chomping grass. Nit whistles a song. He slowly raises his bovine head with its curlicue horns and looks at her, crying.

Toey died a few months ago and was buried alongside one of the fields where he labored nearly all his life.

The World's Fastest Elephant

"The question of the day is: how fast can an elephant run across a level, thirty-meter field when not scared for his (or her) life, but motivated and reasonably fit?"

The person asking this question, and who had ten elephants lined up waiting to provide a possible answer, was John Hutchinson, a recent graduate of the University of California at Berkeley whose post-graduate work brought him to Thailand to find the world's fastest elephant, a query that not only was given credence, but paid for with an academic grant.

My question: is this a question a grown man should even ask?

It's widely conceded that the world's fastest animal is the cheetah, a sleek sprinting machine native to Africa that has been clocked in pursuit of its prey over short distances at an astonishing 68 miles (110 kilometers) per hour.

The pronghorn antelope, another African resident, comes in second at 61 mph (98 kph), not quite fast enough to escape a cheetah's pursuit, except that the antelope is more suited for longer runs.

Other maximum speeds, most of them measured over a quarter-mile (0.4 km) distance, include the lion and the ostrich at 61 mph (80 kph); quarter horse, 47 mph (76 kph); coyote, 43 mph (69 kph); greyhound, 39 mph (63 kph); domestic rabbit, 35 mph (56 kph); giraffe, 32 mph (51 kph); grizzly bear, 30 mph (48 kph); and man, 26 mph (42 kph). Followed, at some distance, by the squirrel at 12 (19 kph), the domestic pig at 11 (18 kph) and the barnyard chicken at 9 (14 kph).

Back to the elephants and John, who told me he was trying to link evolutionary biology and bio-mechanics, two fields, he assured me, that hadn't been talking to each other lately. Which is what brought us to a field behind Rajamangala Institute of Technology in Surin, Thailand, during that town's Annual Elephant Round-Up.

"What," I asked, "do you do to 'motivate' the elephants?"

John said that on the first day's trials, they tried it both with and without the trainers called *mahouts* on top. They also tried shouting and banging empty plastic water bottles together as they ran behind the elephant. And they positioned other elephants—friends of the animal being tested—at the finish line to give him (or her) something to run toward.

The idea was to get the elephant up to a full gallop when the animal crossed an infra-red beam, starting the clock. Thirty meters and a few seconds later the elephant passed a second beam and the clock stopped. Identical tests with Asian elephants in California showed the fastest to move at four meters per second, or about ten miles per hour. John said he thought that was the limit, a "wall," so to speak, comparable to the four-minute mile that humans once were thought unable to surpass.

Then John met, via the internet, Richard Lair, another Californian, but one who has lived in Thailand for about twenty years and is on the staff of the Thai Elephant Conservation Center in Lampang, a small town about an hour's drive from Chiang Mai. He told John his elephants could, in a manner of speaking, run circles around the ones at the San Francisco Zoo, which is where John had tested his pachyderms while working on his doctorate. That prompted John to find some research money and come to Surin, where, indeed, on the first day's run, he timed an elephant running just short of fifteen miles an hour. You have to understand that for John, this was more exciting than the consultancy he did on *Jurassic Park*.

"The general question is, how does body size affect the range of an animal's movements," John explained when I asked why even bother. "How do big things handle being big? Another question is how do the elephants do what they do, because at fifteen miles per hour, they should, like all other animals, including humans, when running at full speed, have all feet in the air at some point. But elephants always have one foot on the ground."

He said humans were able to perform certain "tricks" to move faster and keep one foot on the ground at all times. Speed-walkers integrated a hip movement that enabled them to walk fast. And then, John added, there was something called "Groucho-running." It was, he said, named for Groucho Marx, who stooped and sort of duck-walked in the movies, enabling him to accelerate his pace and maintain uninterrupted contact with the earth.

"Elephants are doing something we haven't figured out yet," John said. It was, he implied, the challenge of his young academic life.

As we talked, seven spots were painted on each elephant on the side facing the cameras that would record the run—on the top of the shoulder (or scapula), at the shoulder joint, on the elbow and wrists on the front leg, and on the hip, knee and ankle of the rear leg. In this fashion, the movement could later be tracked by drawing stick figures based on the film showing their movement as if in slow motion.

The first elephant was led into position. This was a three-year-old named Pop and he calmly walked the measured distance in a little over twenty seconds, a preliminary timing made with which to compare a gallop. He was then returned to the starting position.

Now, his *mahout* stood behind him with two empty plastic water bottles and started banging them together and screaming. Pop took off, the *mahout* in hot pursuit, still banging and yelling, and the relatively tiny beast was at full gallop when he passed the first light beam, tail curled upward as is always true when elephants run, his fat little legs pumping.

John stepped to the counter and read the finish time. "Four-point-nine-two seconds!" Not a record, but faster than a

California elephant and I could tell that John's heart was beating faster, too.

The second elephant was led to the start position. This was May and she was six and had no interest whatsoever in playing this silly game. She walked both laps.

"We'll give her another chance later," said Richard Lair, diplomatically.

I suggested to John that I thought maybe the reason Thai elephants ran faster than California elephants was the animals in San Francisco led a more sedentary lifestyle.

"That's a good word," said one of John's associates, who stood near the clock with a clipboard. "Sedentary."

"Yes," said John, "but it still doesn't explain how the elephants always keep one foot on the ground."

I said I didn't think it was because the elephants were "Groucho-running."

In fact, the only thing I *was* sure of was that Groucho would've liked to have been there.

Behind the Smiles

Talking Thai, Understanding Englit

I'd tried to learn Thai. I really did. I spent more than a hundred dollars on a set of tapes and a manual the size of a small American city's telephone book. I still have a shelf of how-to books and the pocket-sized Thai-English dictionary I carry around with me is so worn a rubber band is all that holds it together. I even enrolled in a class to learn the language.

In many ways, Thai is far simpler than English, once you learn that the adjectives follow the subject and a couple of other easy rules. There are no prefixes or suffixes, no tenses or plurals, nor any articles. The verbs do not conjugate and there are no genders, as in, say, Spanish and French. And there is no punctuation or capitalization.

That's the good news. The bad news is that there are forty-four consonants, twenty-four vowels (each with a long and short form), and five tones. Because it, like some other Asian languages, is constructed of monosyllabic words, thus limiting the number of combination possibilities, how you say and hear the words determines if you can speak or comprehend it. For example, the syllable *mai* can mean "new," "burn," "wood," "not" or "not?," depending on how it's pronounced. Thus you can say *"Mai mai mai mai mai?"* and mean, "New wood doesn't burn, does it?" If your tonal use is correct.

I'd lived in Thailand for about three years when I started classes and I was the star pupil. I knew many of the rules, was familiar with the *sound* of the language, and had a small vocabulary of common words and phrases. But the class quickly passed me by. The first problem was my hearing loss. I was born tone deaf and that made it impossible for me to hear the words precisely and when I spoke, people often didn't understand, wrinkling their brows and, in some instances, suppressing (or not suppressing) laughter. *Suay* with a rising tone, for instance, meant "beautiful," and with a falling tone "bad fortune." Intellectually, I knew this, but I had trouble making it clear what the hell I was saying.

I also had a more general impairment that required mechanical devices to hear speech of any kind, a loss so great I was growing dependent not only on my battery-operated hearing aids but also on a relatively quiet environment and lip-reading to get by. Bangkok is not known for its relative quiet. And reading lips doesn't help much, either, when the language spoken is other than your own, or English is spoken in a manner that changes the pronunciation and thus the movement of the lips. Tones don't show on the lips, either.

My age was another factor. It was generally agreed that picking up a foreign language was a snap when you were young; children living in multi-lingual households learned two and three tongues simultaneously. But apparently the part of the brain that absorbed and sorted language went on holiday more frequently as age advanced and by the time I arrived in Thailand at fifty-eight, my language learning potential could be described as semi-retired. After two months in class, my instructor said she would welcome my presence for as long as I wished to attend, but...graciously, she left it at that.

It's no surprise that this made communication between my wife Lamyai and me difficult, or that a sort of "pidgin" was invented, comprising English used in truncated and imaginative ways, colored by Thai words and rules. Because many Thais spoke English following Thai structure, the adjective frequently followed the subject, thus I had a friend who referred to my landlady as my "lady land." So it was also in describing familial relationships. When Lamyai said "Papa Mayura," she was talking about her cousin Mayura's father, and when she said "young sister husband Lampong," she was referring to her sister Lampong's husband's younger sister. After a while, such "backwards" construction was no problem for me.

Another verbal characteristic was the linking of words in the way Thais ran all their words together in a written sentence. Where in the West someone might greet another saying, "Hot enough for you?" Lamyai exclaimed "Hottoomuch-PapaIwantdie!" A limited vocabularly similarly led to pasting two or three words together to convey a longer message; thus, when she bought school supplies and uniforms for the children, the news was described as "buybookshirt." Sometimes the words strung together were so creative I didn't want to correct her. For instance, she didn't know the word for the "balcony" that fronted the second level of our home, so she said, "papasitdown-drinkbeer," a word/phrase crafted to describe what I was known to do there somewhat more than occasionally.

Further, there was a kindness that gentled some of her messages. I remember Lamyai asking, "Papa, take shower?" and my replying, "No." Lamyai then said, "Maybe Papa not happy not take shower." Someone in the West might have conveyed the same message by saying, "You stink! Take a bath!"

I wasn't alone with pronunciation problems. Thais had them, too. The letter "s" actually presented multiple challenges. Appearing at the start of a word, as in Sukhumvit, the name of the main street in my neighborhood, it began with the sibilance familiar to all. But when the "s" came at the end of the word, inasmuch as Thais don't have any words that end with that sound, it disappeared—my last name was, therefore, pronounced Hopkin—or it was turned into a "t" or "k." Thus, I understood "but" meant "bus," "Jonat" and "Kritee" were the names of two popular *farang* singers of Thai songs named Jonas and Kristy, and when Lamyai said "kit" and "sek," she was saying "kiss" and "sex." As in: "LamyaiwantsekPapatoomuch!" Finally, when an "l" appeared at the end of the word, it became an "n," as in

Orienten Hoten, and an "r" sometimes became an "l," for example, "loom," or disappeared altogether, as when the Central Department Store became "Centen."

Add the charming tendency to put vocal emphasis on a word's last syllable, thus my surname actually was pronounced Hop-KIN, tennis became "ten-NIT," banana became "ba-na-NAH," and my first name was "Jer-EE." Further, an "a" was added to some words, so that steak was voiced "sa-TEAK", small became "sa-MALL, sweet was mouthed "sa-WEET," and the Land of Smiles was shortened and lengthened simultaneously, becoming "Land of Sa-MILE."

Teachers of English in Thailand called all this "Thai-glish" or "Tinglish."

Initially, I figured that for Lamyai, as for myself, that while there was far more to language than stringing words together, vocabulary was more important than pronunciation and tone. Thus, I carried my dictionary around with me and was always asking, "What's the Thai word?" as Lamyai asked me, "How say Eng-LIT?" At the same time, I hoped that the situational context of what I was saying would make up for the way I mangled the ups and downs of the way Thai words were correctly vocalized.

In time, I came to understand Lamyai most of the time fairly easily, as her sometimes imaginative set phrases became a part of my own vocabulary. When she'd had one too many gin-and-tonics and pointed to her head with a finger and said, "Litten bit woo-woo-woo," the meaning was not lost on me. Later, this was replaced with "litten bit dlunk," but I didn't consider that an improvement.

When I dropped my own conversational patterns and vocabulary down to her level, I wasn't doing her any favors, however much it contributed to uninterrupted conversational flow. I even mispronounced some of the words as she did, saying "hab" for "have" and using the words "upstairs" and "downstairs" for "up" and "down," etc. When I returned from a two-week trip to Burma with a friend and he'd given her a report, she told me, "Greg say talk about Lamyai toomuchtoomuch. TalkaboutLamyai.

TalkaboutPhaithoon. Talk-aboutPok. TalkaboutMamaLamyai. Talkabouthou(se). Toomuchtoomuch. Greg say." The error was that in letting this go uncorrected, I may have been aiding communication in the short term—whereas constant corrections to her speech or proper usage on my part would have slowed it—in the long run, it was a mistake.

One more factor contributing to our conversational success was that unlike many Thais with limited English, Lamyai was not shy about using what facility she had. If she knew, say, five-hundred English words, as soon as we were within conversational range (or on the phone) following any separation, she'd use at least four hundred of them four or five times apiece within the first five minutes. Many Thais, even when they actually spoke English well, were too insecure to speak at all to a *farang*. Lamyai, on the other hand, couldn't wait to communicate all her news in my language and didn't want to stop, the words tumbling forth in the manner of someone running downhill, moving faster and faster, until finally she stumbled and fell silent, ending many such raps with a pause followed by the phrase, "Don't know Eng-LIT." Together we then attempted to discover the word or phrase she wanted to vocalize, me searching (usually in vain) in my Thai-English dictionary, while Lamyai remained silent, frustrated.

We also depended on sign and body language and I sometimes found myself drawing pictures in my pocket notebook. Following my son's visit, he told family and friends back in the States that Lamyai spoke English about as well as a second grader and he told me that he thought that was one of the reasons we got on so well: we tried harder to communicate and for so long as the motivation to do so remained, we'd probably do okay.

Kreng Jai

My mother always said that a week was incomplete until you'd worked in the garden and got dirt under your fingernails, so when I fell in love with a rice farmer's daughter and, later on as we planned to marry and built a house on the family farm, I looked forward to getting my hands into the soil, just as my mama advised.

Soon after we moved into the house, Lamyai decided to put in some fruit and vegetable gardens, to thin some old banana patches on the property and move a hundred of the young trees to another piece of land nearby. (She would then add two hundred pineapple plants between the trees and five hundred potato plants.) As Lamyai, her mother, her siblings, her two children and youngest brother all pitched in to dig up and move the bananas, I figured I'd just join in.

Boy, was I wrong! Not only did I not know what I was doing, my assistance was rebuffed. As I took up a machete to trim the leaves of the trees before replanting, I used the wrong (dull) side of the blade, causing several of those present to hide their laughter behind their hands. I knew they weren't laughing at me, but embarrassed by my mistake; I had learned that the Thai response to embarrassment was laughter.

What I *didn't* realize, until Lamyai took me aside later, was that no matter how much I wanted to help, my "status" in the family dictated that I stand aside. It was, she said, *kreng jai*. And what, I asked, was that? She explained, saying that I was older, a foreigner, wealthier, better educated and et cetera and as such I was entitled to a kind and level of respect that, ironically, "kept me in my place."

Kreng jai may be one of the slipperiest and stickiest aspects of Thai culture for a westerner to grasp, and one of the most difficult aspects of Thai character for him or her to accept. It is, as Chrisopher G. Moore explains in his book *Heart Talk* (1992), "a mingling of reverence, respect, deference, homage and fear—which every Thai person feels toward someone who is their senior, their boss, their teacher, mother and father, a police officer or towards those who are perceived to be a member of a higher class."

Mont Redmond, another foreign author, writing in *Wondering into Thai Culture* (1998), saw it the same way, saying "this fear/consideration has produced some of the most adept and elegant manners on the face of this Earth. It is the disappearance of this restraint, and not its somewhat suffocating presence, which is bringing about the ruin of Thailand we see all around us today. Remove the consideration, and you have *coups d'etat*, corruption, and exploitation. Remove the fear, and you have profligacy, crime, and cultural collapse. Offense is everywhere, but fewer and fewer can gain leverage for redress with their feelings alone. As Thais lose the art of making small sacrifices to achieve long-term advantages—the essence of *kwam kreng chai* and diplomacy alike—the clumsy Western machinery of legislation, litigation and demonstration will occupy by default a place reserved in Thai hearts for the subtlest forms of blame, shame, and well-deserved fame."

In time, I learned that that was, unsurprisingly, a foreign point of view, and as a foreigner I still haven't totally discarded it. The way I saw it, *kreng jai* was a hangover from the feudal system that still influences so much modern Thai behavior—resembling in unsettling ways the class system that clings to English life and the caste system that still rules India, and in a less severe way, the kowtowing of China. Because *kreng jai* determined, or at least colored, virtually all relationships, I saw it as a way to open wide the doors to frequent and easy abuse.

Kreng jai is learned from childhood. Within the family, the order of birth is important. There are separate words for older and younger siblings, and the older is the most respected, regardless of whether he or she has earned that respect. Thus, if you are the third born child, you are "superior" to any children born after you and you defer to Numbers One and Two. Similarly, of course, parents and grandparents and uncles and aunts also are automatic beneficiaries of *kreng jai.*

It additionally affects relationships between the sexes. Thailand is, like too many countries in the world, sexist, and it is the male who is valued more than the female, and therefore given more "respect." Along with more choices, higher salaries, and so on.

Similarly, when two Thai strangers meet, where they fit into Thailand's complex social scheme may be the first order of business. Sometimes appearance tells all, as it would if one is obviously older than the other. Wardrobe may do it, too, as will accent; the dialects characteristically found in the northeastern and southern parts of the country may establish social place as quickly as Cockney would in Oxford, or one of the Cantonese variations likely will in Mandarin Beijing. A person's home town or school can do the same. Similar biases exist around the world.

Having a powerful father or a strong political connection in Thailand is another sure path to entitlement, and for some a kind of immunity. Consider the case of a former police captain and onetime Cabinet Minister whose two sons had a reputation for beating up people in pubs and were charged with forging documents to evade military service. When one of them was accused of shooting a cop dead in a pub, despite the prosecution's claim to have more than sixty eye-witnesses, the young man went free as earlier testimony was reversed and witnesses suffered loss of memory. Nor was anyone surprised when the sons of one of Thailand's godfathers of crime were elected to Parliament.

Possessions and personal extravagances are another means of acquiring *kreng jai.* Thus, Thailand during the boom years became one of the world's top markets for Mercedes-Benz automobiles (with BMWs and Volvos not far behind) and the single best market on the planet for Johnny Walker Black Label Scotch. A prominent politician openly bragged to a newspaper reporter that he only felt comfortable when wearing suits designed by Armani, shirts by Versace, neckties by Lanvin and Valentino, shoes by Tettoni, and belts by Louis Vuitton. Nor was it unknown for the newly rich to have surrounding trees removed after building a showcase house because they blocked others from viewing the magnificent edifice.

It's pointless to try to explain that all men and women are created equal, as I repeatedly do with Lamyai, with no success whatsoever—because in Thailand, as in George Orwell's novel, *Animal Farm*, "All animals are created equal, but some are more equal than others." It is as ingrained and automatic in social situations as the deferential hands-held-together *wai* helps define everyday greetings.

Sometimes this is carried to what westerners might call extremes. Kriengsak Niratpattanasai, an executive at DBS Thai Danu Bank, writes a weekly column in the *Bangkok Post* and in 2004 published a book, *Bridging the Gap: Managing the Cross-Cultural Workplace in Thailand*. In it, he told a story from his weekly column in the *Bangkok Post*, "Bridging the Gap" (Mar. 1, 2002) about a businessman who "loved to drive his car on provincial business trips. Aware that his health was weak, he always brought his driver as a contingency plan. On one trip the car crashed, the businessman died and his driver was seriously injured. Questioned by police after he recovered, the driver said that his boss often drove too fast and on that day visibility was poor. The driver confessed that he was too *kreng jai* to advise his boss to slow down."

A similar story is known to all in Thailand. When a princess fell out of a boat and drowned, dozens stood by and did nothing. The taboo about physically touching anyone from the royal family was so ingrained in the population at that time, no one felt it permissible to try to help because it would've meant making contact. This same deference paid to the royal family still causes servants and many others to fall to their hands and knees and crawl when in their presence today, although this practice was forbidden by an earlier monarch nearly a hundred years ago.

It's easy for a foreigner to criticize, yet many who have lived here longer than I praise *kreng jai*. In *Heart Talk*, Christopher Moore credits it with helping create "the incredible degree of politeness and civility found in exchanges between Thai people." William Klausner, author of *Reflections on Thai Culture* (1991), said, "There is no English word for *kreng jai* because the *farang* don't *kreng jai*." And in his book, *Bridging the Gap*, Kriengsak Niratpattanasai insists that whatever abuses may result, the phrase means "being aware of another person's feelings, helping others save face, and showing respect and consideration. More than behavior, it is a core Thai value." And, he said, when "applied wisely, it can bring success in daily life."

Not long ago, how the pendulum swings both ways was shown within my extended Thai family. My wife's youngest sister, her husband, and their three-year-old son shared a room in Bangkok, where they worked in the garment industry. They worked different hours, so someone was at home with the boy at all times. As my wife, Lamyai, told the story, a number of her sister's husband's relatives started visiting the room on a daily basis, drinking and talking noisily and filling the small space with cigarette smoke. They weren't, said Lamyai, showing her sister *kreng jai*, were not giving her time alone with her son and were creating an annoying, unhealthy environment.

Why didn't Lamyai's sister tell the boors to leave? *Kreng jai*. They were her husband's relatives. Why, I asked, didn't she say something to her husband? *Kreng jai* again. A good wife didn't complain.

I will add this, however. After Lamyai and I married, and I'd been around for a couple of years, I was welcomed in the garden.

May the Force Be With You

Not long after I moved to Thailand, I witnessed a fender bender involving a taxi and a car. The drivers, both male, emerged from their vehicles like angry animals. It was clear they were going to settle the matter of responsibility on the spot.

Then something happened that I didn't understand. The cab driver quickly removed his shirt and just stood there, his torso bared to the mid-day Bangkok sun, shimmering with elaborate tattoos, his back covered in Thai script. The other driver ran to his car and drove away. What I had witnessed, a friend later explained, was the magic of Thai tattoos. The driver who ran knew he couldn't win a fistfight with a man with that much supernatural protection.

When my wife Lamyai and I spent a long weekend in Hua Hin, staying in a bungalow near the beach, before we went to bed that night she put a one-baht coin under each pillow and when we left a few days later she said, "Good-bye, house. Thank you for sleep. See you next time." She told me that both actions, unheard of in the part of the world I came from (the United States), were to appease the spirits in the house and the land on which it sat.

To the outsider, Thailand may look like a modern country, with cable television available in all seventy-six provinces, internet cafes virtually everywhere you look, and what surely might be Asia's greatest saturation of mobile phones. The vast majority of Thais also are Buddhist, or say they are, yet over centuries, the national religion has been thrown into a spiritual blender with a much older belief in supernatural forces. Thus, there are tens of thousands of men and women who make their living as astrologers, numerologists, fortune-tellers, shamans, *feng shui* experts, and other types of spiritualists, and tens of millions of people with computers and cell phones who follow them.

In the West, many disparage such beliefs, calling them groundless superstition and irrational bunk. Yet, it is helpful to remember that while it is true that the wife of Chavalit Yongchaiyudh, a prime minister in the 1990s, worshipped Rahu, the god of darkness who is said to swallow the moon during eclipses, it also is true that the wife of American President Ronald Reagan consulted an astrologer and then advised her husband accordingly, and that 60 percent of all Americans say they read their horoscope regularly.

John Hoskin explained in his book *The Supernatural in Thai Life* (1993) that Buddhism "is concerned primarily with man's ultimate release from suffering, from the cycle of death and rebirth. As such, it does not address mundane problems. At the same time, it is a tolerant faith, not necessarily negating additional beliefs that may be deemed relevant and beneficial to daily well-being. Accordingly, the Thais have inherited from their animistic ancestors a host of beliefs in supernatural powers that interact with ordinary life. Rather than contradict Buddhism, these convictions are held in such a close and complex relationship with the national religion that an outsider can scarcely differentiate the dual elements." In other words, the Thais aren't taking any chances, and for the man with all the tattoos, they certainly protected him the day I watched him take off his shirt. Nor did any unpleasant incidents occur during our stay in Hua Hin.

It's probably accurate to say that a majority of Thais believe strongly in the protective power of tattoos, amulets and blessings given by monks. Lottery tickets are purchased on the basis of numbers remembered from dreams or divined while visiting a "magical" tree or shrine. Family members and village elders tie white and gold thread around others' wrists to bring good luck. Caged birds are released for the same reason.

The omnipresence of spirit houses in Thailand—you'll even see them outside modern skyscrapers—stems from the belief that prior to human occupation, spirits inhabited the site and lest they become angry and bring misfortune to the new arrivals, they must be given a home of their own and daily recognition in the form of incense, food, and drink. (Often a bottle of pop with a straw in it, which always makes me smile. As does the occasional hog's head or kilogram of bacon, two other frequent offerings.)

Every year when new vehicle license plates are issued, fiercely competitive auctions are held for those with "auspicious" numbers. A plate with "9999" has been sold for as much as US$100,000, the cash from these sales going to the Land Transport Department's road safety fund. Ordinary, everyday currency with "lucky" numbers is sold in shops for hundreds of times the face value.

A shrine outside a Bangkok department store is visited by teenagers every day from nine to ten in the morning so that the "god" residing there may bless and help the lovesick. Those seeking good luck in school or in the office or any other endeavor including winning the lottery go to the Erawan Shrine, lighting candles, offering flowers, burning incense, and paying women in traditional costume to dance…then perhaps buy a lottery ticket from one of the many vendors outside the gates. Others on Tuesday nights visit a bronze stature of Rama V, the beloved King Chulalongkorn who ruled as absolute monarch from 1868 to 1910; many believe he will return to rule Thailand again, saving it from its many sins and weaknesses.

Ghosts are a constant, a staple in magazines, books, movies and television soap operas as well as in daily life. When Lamyai's brother Pairuen died in a motorcycle accident, an elaborate ceremony was performed at the time of his cremation to reunite his body with his spirit, which was believed to have been jarred from his body by the violence of this death. This was followed by a seven-day-long "ghost watch," with some twenty or so relatives and neighbors spending the nights in our house; several reported sightings and the next week the house in which he died was dismantled and sold as scrap lumber.

I remember going to a bar one night to find the movie *Ghost* on TV. When this film, starring Patrick Swayze and Demi Moore, was released in Thailand, it became the most popular foreign motion picture of the year. Now I watched all the Thai women in the bar, frozen in place, mesmerized, ignoring customers as they sat staring at the box over the disc jockey's booth, or stood nearly motionless on the stage; business practically halted until the movie ended. Another time I took an ailing computer to be examined and after half an hour the repair man said he couldn't find anything to fix, thus my problem must be a *phee*, or ghost. (We in the West fear viruses; Thais fear ghosts.) Some other examples:

- In 1991, when Banharn Silpa-archa was finance minister, he ordered the removal of two wooden elephants from the front door of the Finance Ministry to a temple on the advice of a fortune-teller who said elephants would endanger his position; the surname "Silpa-archa" means "horse" and as everyone must know, pachyderms trump equines every time. Six years later, the new finance minister moved them back, hoping the move would cure the economic problems the country was having. A month after that, the baht was devalued and the economy of the entire region crashed.

- In 1996, when astrologers told Banharn that bad stars had moved into his horoscope, he changed the date of his birth from July 20, 1932, to August 19, 1932, so he could be a Leo rather than a Cancer. A government spokesman explained that the traditional Thai way of counting days differed from the international method and said that this was the source of the error. Someone else pointed out that Leo was the sign of several previous prime ministers who served long terms, implying that was the real motive. Banharn lasted a year.

- In 1995, The *Nation* reported that nearly one-third of all members of Parliament collected amulets as a hobby. Some of the amulets were said to be five-hundred-years old and worth as much as US$400,000.

- In 1997, the wife of Prime Minister Chavalit Yongchaiyudh insisted she and her husband moved house when a fortune-teller told her that a leak in the roof and a crack in the wall of their present abode would cause troubles for the family. She and her husband then conducted a five-hour-long religious rite—she worships Rahu, remember—to dispel the bad luck during the time they moved temporarily into another house while the leak was fixed. It was reported that they both wore black and burned more than one hundred black candles to say farewell to the god who, presumably, remained behind to supervise repairs.

- In 2000, the army demolished an official residence for top brass because it was believed to be shrouded in ill omen; apparently bad luck had come to those who lived there. A new house was built at a cost of US$125,000.

- In 2003, it was widely reported that the 443 Thai military personnel sent to Iraq to support America's war took with them more than six thousand Buddha amulets, pieces of blessed cloth and sacred phallic images to assure their safety. The following year, all but two of the men returned.

- In 2004, when two historians cast doubt on the authenticity of an inscription reportedly found by a thirteenth century king in Sukhothai, some five thousand residents of the former capital gathered in front of the monarch's statue and burned chilis and salt in an act of protest, believing the ancient rite would consign the historians to a purgatory of endless flame.

It all sounded to my "rational" Western mind like something you encountered in a novel by Stephen King and I thought a good argument could be made for the benefits that would come if superstition were somehow to vanish from the earth. I also acknowledged the possibility that the world might be thrown into chaos if these belief systems disappeared overnight...and that it would be a much less colorful place. I further knew that one of the quickest ways to get into trouble in Thailand was to examine things logically.

As reported in the *Bangkok Post* (Sep. 27, 2004), some people believed that delays in construction of Bangkok's new international airport stemmed "not from man-made errors but supernatural phenomena." Srisook Chandrangsu, the transport permanent secretary and chairman of the New Bangkok International Airport was quoted as saying he thought the absence of a proper shrine might have caused many of the problems. When a shrine was constructed to house all the deities in the area and troubles continued, experts recommended a larger shrine.

"A Thai-style pavilion was also built to house a foundation stone laid at the site by His Majesty the King," the *Post* continued. "Before, the foundation stone was stored in a poorly illuminated place, which some believed was unbefitting, and might also have caused troubles. It has now been placed in a brightly lit place.

"Mr. Srisook said he was confronted with countless problems when he was asked to supervise the project. But after he placed a Buddha image in a meeting room...many of the problems and arguments were peacefully resolved. 'We have to believe that supernatural powers are real,' said Mr. Srisook."

However mismatched these notions and practices may be to mine, I do not scoff. The Thai friend who explained the incident involving the tattooed taxi driver also gave me some good advice. "Not your country," she said. "Don't want to see you falling down." Her English may have been somewhat quirky, but her message made good sense.

Almost as much as my crossing my fingers, knocking on wood, throwing salt over my shoulder, worrying about broken mirrors and black cats, walking under ladders, and numbering the floors in high-rise buildings so they skipped "13."

Thai Time

Nittaya Phanthachat, a friend who stayed with me from time to time when she was visiting Bangkok (she had a home in Chon Buri), told me one morning as she left my flat that she'd be back in time for us to have dinner together.

She called at four o'clock and said she was running late, but promised to be back at eight. We still had time for dinner. No problem.

She finally showed up two days later.

Was I angry? No, not really. I was concerned about her safety and health, as anyone might be, but the worry, if that's the correct word, was tempered by the knowledge that Thais don't have the same concept of time that westerners do. In fact, not only is it different, to many of us raised in the West, it makes no sense at all, as if we'd suddenly awoken on a planet that moved around the Sun at an unfamiliar speed, with, literally, a different sense of gravity.

Consider being on Mercury. Mercury moves with great dispatch in its journey around the Sun, averaging approximately thirty miles per second and completing its circuit in about eighty-eight Earth days. Yet, this tiniest planet and the closest in the solar system to the Sun, rotates upon its axis so slowly, the time from one sunrise to the next is equal to about 176 days on Earth. Try setting your Swatch or Rolex to that. And think about how long Happy Hour might be.

Compared to Mercury's, Nittaya's sense of time was easy to grasp. I'd moved to Thailand after living for many years in Hawaii, where there was something called "Hawaiian time," a complex system of measuring the duration of all existence, past, present, and future, that was defined by a single word: late. So, "Thai time" was just another excuse. Yes?

That's the *farang* point of view, of course. Hawaiians are never late, according to "Hawaiian time." Identically, Thais are never late. They've merely been delayed, or perhaps distracted. The ancient Greeks, in whom *farangs* perhaps put too much faith, advised us to be "ruled by time, the wisest counselor of all" and while that may have worked in ancient Greece and back home in the twenty-first-century United States, as any fool knows, Greek thought is not included in the Thai primary school curriculum. End of discussion.

A little harder to grasp is the Thai's understanding of "time" as a concept. For this part of my tale, you need some patience, and perhaps a beer or a nice cuppa tea, so put this book down and get the drink of your choice—take your time!—and then take a deep breath and for just a minute, no longer, I promise, let me turn you over to William J. Klausner, a *farang* who came to Thailand in 1955, lived for a year in a village in Isan, was an editor of the annual publication of the Buddhist Association of Thailand, and taught at both Thammasat and Chulalongkorn Universities. A wise man.

"One of the central concepts of Buddhist philosophy is *ani-cang*: the transitory nature of the material world in which we live; the uncertainty and impermanence of all," he wrote in *Reflections on Thai Culture* (1981). "The Thai version of *mañana*, the tried and true answer to failed appointments and the lack of successful and timely task completion, is *mai pen rai*, or 'it is nothing,' 'never mind,'" he continued. "Sociologists have referred to the present-oriented aspect of Thai behavior and personality. Certainly, the Thai find more psychological fulfillment in the chase than in the attainment. It is the voyage, the journey that is fun; the end result is less important. Thus, one shouldn't be too concerned if one is some minutes or some hours late."

Did everybody follow that? *Mai pen rai.*

It all has to do with Oriental thought, and most specifically the Buddhist vision of constant and cosmic flow. That thing about the wheel that keeps turning without any real beginning and end. I don't know for sure, but this may be one of the reasons the Thai language doesn't have any tenses, and for that alone I'm grateful. While English speakers have the audacity to include such things as "past perfect" and "future perfect" but no "present perfect" in the way they speak. If you ask me, it's not a matter of Thai time making no sense, it's the other way around.

As for my friend Nittaya, she'd just run into some friends with whom she caught a bus to Bang Saen for a day at the beach. So her return to my flat two days late merely meant we had dinner on Tuesday instead of Sunday. No problem.

Where a Dildo Means Good Luck

BANG BANG BANG BANG BANG!

It's nine o'clock at night at the Hog's Breath Saloon when suddenly there's a horrific pounding, as if a carpenter has been sent to remodel the place just as the first of the leggy darlings are climbing onto the stage to dance.

No. It's only the nightly *phlad kikh* ceremony, which begins the evening's fun. In Thailand, the *phlad kikh* (translation: "honorable surrogate penis") is a phallic symbol usually carved from wood that is believed to bring the owner—or even someone who touches it—luck. It may be small enough to hide in a pocket or wear on a chain around the neck, as big around as a man's arm or leg, or even several meters in length.

The one in play at the Hog's Breath is about thirty centimeters/twelve-inches long and eight centimeters/three inches in diameter, and it's being banged against the bar's open front door frame, top, bottom, and sides. The scantily clad young lady holding the object now dunks the head into a glass of Thai whisky, draws a series of circles on the floor, then bangs the floor and door frame again.

As she does this, a dozen other dancers line up behind her, extending into the bar, their legs spread wide. Now the lead bar girl bends forward at the waist, removes the glass, and slides the big wooden dick along the floor between all the high heels behind her. All the girls scream in mock ecstacy.

The *phlad kikh* is returned to the young woman in charge of the ceremony, and she now makes a circuit of the bar, touching its rounded head to the loins of each girl in the bar, an act that brings more squeals. And from the male customers in attendance laughter and encouragement.

This is no joke, or at least not entirely. In Thailand, the phallic symbol and its worship is regarded seriously, by bar girls and millions more. However it may seem to an outsider, especially in the Christian world, the *phlad kikh's* origins are as legitimate as they are worldwide, going back to cave drawings of Paleolithic times, embracing the cult of Priapus in classical times, through witchcraft and paganism in early Europe, to the sensual religions of the East, as epitomized today by the Shiva lingam in India, found in every Hindu temple and in many city squares—most often as a symbol of fertility. Though Christian moralism almost totally banished phallic worship, Joshua and Solomon paid homage to a stone in the *Bible* (1 Kings, 3,4) and there is a similar report of Jacob's prayers to a pillar in Genesis 28. Not everyone would agree, but the architecture of Islamic mosques bears more than a passing resemblance to phalluses.

For a long time it was thought that it was from India that Thailand got its phallic worship, but archeologists have since discovered similar images painted on pots dating from about 1000 BC, long before Indian influence had any real impact on Southeast Asia. Again as a symbol of fertility.

Unknown to most of its guests, on the grounds of the Nai Lert Park Hotel (formerly the Bangkok Hilton) there is a small shrine dedicated to phallic offerings, at the north end of the property beside the Saen Saep Canal behind the parking structure. Here, about a hundred *phlad kikh* crafted from various materials are displayed, ranging up to three meters in length and arranged around a spirit house built by millionaire businessman Nai Lert to honor Jao Mae Thapthim, a female deity thought to reside in the old banyan tree nearby. It's believed that a woman who made an offering soon got pregnant, thus the shrine is mainly visited by childless women who offer incense, flowers, food and cigarettes.

Of course, pregnancy is not what the girls at the Hog's Breath want. (May all the animist gods forbid!) There, if you're pregnant, you're out of work.

Nor do they want the protection from evil and snake bites that the amulet was thought to bring small boys who, once upon a time, carried the amulets in their pockets before setting off for school, or worn on a waist string under their clothing, off-center from the real penis in the belief they would attract and absorb any injury directed toward the generative organs.

Early styles of *phlad kikh* bear inscribed invocations, entreaties and praises to Shiva; later ones combine these with appeals and prayers to Buddha; modern ones bear uniformly Buddhist inscriptions written in an ancient script that cannot be read by contemporary Thais. Amulets carved from wood, bone and horn once were made by monks who specialized in their manufacture and the respect given an amulet was connected to the charisma and reputation of its creator.

Today, the greatest number are mass produced for the tourist trade, in wood, bronze, pewter and plastic. Some depict Hanuman, the Monkey God of the Hindus, crouched upon an erect penis, his tail arched over his back. Tigers are given human shafts double the length of the animal. Demons that look like something from a horror movie from Hollywood threaten to commit fellatio with pointy teeth. On others, women straddle an outsized penis, wearing a smile and a polka-dotted bikini.

Amulet markets in Bangkok and elsewhere still offer the real thing, but at most street stalls the charms are now as laughable as they are divorced from authenticity, and the titillation factor has led to most being hugely overpriced.

For the bar girls and for most Thais today, the *phlad kikh* is used to summon good luck and, in places of business, a rich and generous customer. Today all over Thailand, they may be seen in places of commerce, next to the cash register in a mom and pop store or nestled in a pile of knockoff designer gear at a street vendor's stall, in the still unswerving belief that its presence will be good for business, or at the very least cannot hurt. I once saw one the size of a grown man's thigh mounted between the front seats of a Bangkok taxi.

"How's business?" I asked.

He said it was terrible.

A Cool Heart in a Hot Climate

I was walking along Sukhumvit Road to my bank when a motorcycle gave me a bump as it passed. I was on the sidewalk when this happened and I wasn't pleased, and inasmuch as it was the second time in a week that a motorcyclist had run into me on what Thais call a "footpath," I decided to take action. Motorcylists had been using the sidewalks as if they were another lane in the road for a while and I figured it was time to do something about it.

I ran behind the bike, catching up in about half a block when the driver parked next to the bank. I reached him just as he placed his helmet on one of his handle grips. He saw me and looked somewhat chagrined.

"Sorry, sorry, sorry," he said.

"Not good enough!" I yelled, and I grabbed his helmet and threw it into the street just as a bus passed, running over it. Then, realizing what a stupid mistake I'd made, I turned about and ran, anxious to get away before he beat the hell out of me or pulled a gun and shot me dead. If that had happened—and, happily, it didn't—a dozen witnesses would've told police, "This *farang* came out of nowhere and attacked him..."

I can't remember, and wouldn't want to tell you if I could, how many times I've lost my temper since moving to Thailand. But let me recall, as an exercise in humility, one other incident. This occurred when my computer was giving me fits and I took it to a repair shop, where the owner called the Apple distributor and before I knew it I was yelling at someone at the other end of the phone line, and he hung up on me. I told (not asked) the shop owner to call the man back, which he politely did. The man told the shop owner that he didn't want to talk to me, I was *jai rawn*, I had a hot heart.

I grabbed the phone and said, "What do you mean you won't talk to me? I need help."

There was a silence at the other end of the line.

After a moment, I apologized. "Look, I'm really sorry," I said. "And I do need your help." There was another long pause and he told me to bring the computer to him. When I did, he said it would take a couple of weeks to fix my computer and in the meantime, he said, he'd give me an old one, which he then spent nearly an hour programming for my use. It doesn't need saying that I felt well and appropriately demoted in the karmic food chain.

Sadly, this is a typical *farang* way of reacting to the many frustrations encountered on a daily basis and as is true nearly everywhere, it seldom gets you anywhere. Certainly, it makes no friends, least of all in the Land of Smiles, where an open display of emotion is considered extremely poor form.

It is okay to laugh, but even then it's best if you hide your laughter behind your hand. Even wailing with grief is acceptable, under very specific circumstances. A smile, of course, is even encouraged. And now that Thailand has joined the league of football nations, when the Thai team—or Manchester United, the country's favorite, for reasons I don't comprehend—scores a point, it is definitely alright to cheer and pound on the bar top and fall off the stool slobbering drunk. But an open loss of temper is not acceptable. Ever.

We're talking about *jai yen*, which literally means a "cool heart." A heart that isn't hot. *Jai yen* has been, and continues to be, the hardest lesson for me to learn, and I recognize the possibility, maybe the likelihood, that I may never completely embrace the concept—that, instead, I'll always be one of those unpredictable, explosive assholes that the Thais reluctantly but graciously put up with.

Actually, they don't have to put up with us, and that they do is a sign of their own *jai yen*.

This doesn't mean that Thais don't lose their temper. They do. Getting mad and shooting someone is an efficient and popular way to handle business and personal conflicts. (You just don't show your anger and you hire someone else to do the shooting, usually from the back of a motorbike.) Thailand also has a growing incidence of road rage and a high rate of rape, wife-beating and child abuse, so it's clear that *jai rawn* is not exclusively a *farang* experience. Yet when it comes to in-your-face, public shouting matches, there is nothing in the Kingdom to compare to life back home in the West, where epithets, curses and tantrums seem an essential part of every day.

My friend Chris Moore, who wrote a book exploring the language use of *jai* or heart, *Heart Talk* (1992), includes *jai yen* in a chapter devoted to self-control. "In Thai culture," he wrote, "considerable virtue is attached to the ability of a person to exercise restraint over feelings of rage, anger or upset. The idea is not to be drawn into an emotional reaction when provoked. There is an attempt to avoid confrontations and the heated exchange."

The ideal is to aspire to calmness, concentration and self-control. Thus there are, referring again to Chris's book, phrases (concepts) such as *hak jai* (restrain heart), *yap yang chang jai* (stop heart), *khom jai* (control heart), *sangop jai* and *rangap jai* (calm heart). The goal is to show *jai yen*, what Chris calls "the Thai equivalent of an English metaphor, a stiff upper lip." For example, he says, when a woman is told by a friend that her husband was seen with another woman, the woman doesn't show any emotion. (What happens later between the woman and her husband is of no concern of ours, though it may defy the concept of *jai yen*.)

Farangs not only find this difficult, they may say it's hypocritical. If you feel something, show it and say it, is the *farang* way. Excessive politeness, especially when it doesn't reflect true feeling, is false and is a disservice to all.

Maybe so, but probably not. Still, the next time a motorcyclist slams into me on a sidewalk, I think I may have a hard time telling him to have a nice day.

Fun & Games in the Slum

Father Joe Maier was telling a story about the children in the Bangkok slums where he's lived and worked for more than thirty years. It was an inspirational story, the sort Catholic priests like to tell. Father Joe runs an organization with thirty-four kindergartens, more than a hundred soccer teams, five shelters for street kids, a medical clinic, Bangkok's only AIDS hospice and a paralegal team that represents two hundred kids in courts and police stations a month, so he has many such stories. Many are distressing—no surprise there—but this is a story about *sanuk*, the Thai word for "fun."

Near Father Joe's house was a large open space where tenwheel trucks parked between long hauls, close to where pigs were butchered for Bangkok's markets. There was no drainage system and rain and diesel oil and other waste collected in puddles. Yet it was here that the neighborhood children played, because there were no parks or playgrounds, nor any space adjacent to the tired wood shacks knocked up against one another and connected by dodgy pathways just wide enough for two people or one motorcycle to pass.

Near where we stood, three girls were jumping rope—two holding a "rope" made of rubber bands strung together, the third jumping. "Notice that they're in the puddles of oil and filth," said the sixty-year-old American priest, "and that they've taken off their shoes. Do you know why? They say they can jump higher without anything on their feet. Which is the object of the game: to jump higher." The death squeals of the hogs rang through the slum in the night. During the day, it was the laughter of the kids.

One writer about Thai culture described *sanuk* as "the fizz in the soft drink of life. Bottled up by the pressures of face and social calculation," he went on, "it surges to the surface whenever it has a chance." In other words, remaining faithful to this wise man's analogy, it is what an optimist does when life gives him a lemon: he makes lemonade. And so it is in the slums of Bangkok where games can serve as an otherwise grim life's lemonade stand.

Thailand is remarkable in this. If there were an Olympic event called playfulness, Thailand would win gold, silver and bronze every time. And it's not just the children. Is it possible for a day to pass without seeing young men hunkered down on a city sidewalk playing a variation of checkers with bottle caps, or kicking a woven rattan ball called a *takraw* around during a work break that others elsewhere would use to smoke cigarettes? It is as if the Thai sense of play were genetic.

Father Joe, a kind of, well, father figure to more than four thousand Bangkok school children, believes it is in the playgrounds—and truck parking lots—where much of this creative frittering away of leisure time begins. So where better to look for evidence than on Father Joe's turf in Klong Toey, one of Asia's largest and bleakest slums.

Here you can see a game played in many countries, the contest using a fist, an open hand, and two moving fingers to signify stone, paper, and scissors. Two children throw hand signs at each other simultaneously—a fist representing a rock, a flat hand paper, the first two fingers extended and opening and closing like scissors. If both throw the same sign, they try again until they are different. The rule is: stone breaks scissors, but scissors cut paper, and paper covers stone. It is the child's way of deciding who goes first, of tossing a coin when there are no coins.

The form of many games played in Thailand is defined by such economy. When a child's pockets are empty of cash, he or she doesn't pitch one *baht* coins, instead rubber bands are placed on a flat surface and blown with the breath to move them toward a designated line or wall. Thus a game is improvised with something found without cost wherever rubber bands are used to tie off bags of food sold on the street.

In another game, coconut shells are cut in half with a hole drilled in the middle. A piece of string connects the shells together with knots inside each one. Players stand on the shells holding the string with their toes and hands as they move toward a finish line. If your feet touch the ground, you're disqualified and the first two to cross the line race again.

Sticks and stones play a leading role in traditional games. In another race, wooden stakes are driven into the ground an agreed distance apart (usually eight to ten meters) and players form two teams, lining up behind the two stakes. A smaller stick, or baton, is given to each team and when a signal is given, the first player of each team runs around the opposite stake, returning to his team and passing it to the next in line.

In another, players place a small rock on the back of the hand, toss it into the air, then catch it, then do the same with two, catching each rock separately as they fall. Then three, then four, then five if they can, until the players are unable to catch all of the stones before one hits the ground. Miss one and you are out of the game. This continues until a single player remains.

Still other games involve no more effort than drawing a line in the dirt. To play one, it must be a sunny day when a circle is drawn on the ground large enough to hold all the players. One child is selected to be the "giant" and he or she chases the others, trying to step on their shadows. When the giant treads on someone's shadow, that player becomes the new giant and play resumes until everyone decides to play a different game. As is the case in many traditional Thai games, there are no losers and winners. The play is for the sake of play.

In a second game in the same category, players of one team sit on the floor or ground in pairs, back to back and feet to feet, making a circle. Players from a second team try to jump over the first team's legs and into the circle, while the sitters kick up their feet to try to touch the jumpers. If one of the jumpers is successful, his team wins and the two teams change places.

Sadly, such games are not played as widely as once they were, replaced by computer games in the home, video parlors in shopping malls, and other amusements involving expensive equipment. Today, many Thai children race on roller blades, or compete with a machine instead of another child.

It is in the countryside and among the urban poor where *sanuk* in play remains affordable.

The King Swings

When the original King of Swing, Benny Goodman, jammed with the King of Thailand in 1960 in New York and was asked to assess the monarch's talent as a saxophone player, he said His Majesty King Bhumibol Adulyadej apparently already had a career worth hanging on to, but added, "If he needed a job, I'd hire him as a member of my band."

Similarly, the great jazz vibraphonist Lionel Hampton once said, "He is simply the coolest king in the land." So it is no surprise that to mark his fiftieth year on the throne, a number of the world's finest musicians traveled to Thailand to pay tribute by performing His Majesty's musical compositions. In 1996, Bangkok hosted concerts by Herbie Hancock, Wayne Shorter, Thelonius Monk Jr. and Benny Carter, saluting what the *Guinness Book of Records* called "The Longest Reigning Monarch in the World." In addition, two compact discs were released featuring Hucky Eichelmann, a German-born classical guitarist who emigrated to Thailand in 1979, and the Bangkok Symphony Orchestra.

It was at age ten when the future monarch started playing the clarinet on an instrument that was purchased—according to his official history—with savings from his allowance, earned while attending school in Switzerland. At that time, his brother, older by only two years, was king, also living in Switzerland and ruling in absentia.

The young future ruler was formally trained in classical music and on his own played along with gramaphone records imported mainly from the United States. Soprano saxophonist Sidney Bechet, one of the Dixieland pioneers from New Orleans, and alto saxophonist Johnny Hodges of Duke Ellington's swing era band were among his favorites.

His cousin and brother reportedly encouraged him to continue his musical studies and urged him to compose songs in addition to playing them. He wrote his first in 1946, the same year he ascended to the throne, following his brother's death.

For many years, the King gathered some musical friends together for Friday night jam sessions in the palace, broadcasting them on the radio. Usually he performed on the saxophone, less frequently on the clarinet, piano or, rarely, guitar.

In the 1960s in New York, on a cross-country trip to America, he played not only with Goodman and Hampton, but also Louis Armstrong, Gene Krupa and Jack Teagarden, and then went on to California to meet—but not play with—the King of Rock and Roll, Elvis Presley. Many photos of that meeting, on the set of Presley's *G.I. Blues*, are prominently displayed and sold as souvenirs in Bangkok today.

Later, during the war in Vietnam, when American Bob Hope played for American troops, His Majesty invited the comedian's bandleader, Les Brown, and vocalist Patti Page, to play with him at his palace home. His music was also included in a Broadway revue in the 1950s and in 1964, following the introduction of a three-movement ballet, he was named to the Institute of Music and Arts of the City of Vienna, the first Asian composer to be so honored.

Of course, his music was best known at home. Every day at eight a.m. and six p.m., all local television stations in Thailand played the national anthem, which was composed by the King. It was also played before most concerts, movies and sporting events. Joggers in Lumpini Park, Bangkok's largest park, halt when the anthem is broadcast and everywhere, the citizens of the Kingdom stand.

In addition, the King composed the alma maters for three of Thailand's leading universities (Chulalongkorn, Thammasat and Kasetsart), along with love songs, rags and blues, many of which have been recorded by a number of artists. In a popular Bangkok nightclub frequented by jazz and blues fans, over the stage is a huge photograph of the King playing the saxophone, the instrument for which the club is named.

When Hucky Eichelmann moved to Bangkok in 1979 to join the music faculty at Chulalongkorn—after teaching at the University of the Philippines in Manila—his repertoire was limited to Bach, Vivaldi and other classical composers. What he discovered was that the Thai audience for classical guitar—and for classical music, for that matter—was practically nonexistent.

"Then I learned that Thailand's King wrote music, and that the people knew and loved the music, just as they loved the King," Hucky recalled. "So after getting permission from the palace, I recorded an album of ten of the King's songs. A year later, the King called for a command performance and I was formally introduced."

Hucky said 350,000 copies of the album were sold, an astonishing number for a market of Thailand's size. His new tribute to the monarch, called *His Majesty's Blues*, contains fifteen more royal compositions, spanning the range of the King's works, including not only the blues, but also love songs and Dixieland-inspired rags.

"The King's music is good," Hucky said. "He has written some very lyrical things. His patriotic songs are sincere and his ragtime is fun. He is spontaneous, a part of his love for jazz. There is in his repertoire, as in his reign, a sense of balance."

It's been many years since His Majesty traveled abroad with his saxophone. Yet, his music still circles the earth as Hucky spends about half of each year touring Europe and the Americas, taking the royal repertoire to a growing audience. "I tell them that there's a king out there writing and playing music," he said. "At first, they don't believe it. So I play a few of the songs and the people really enjoy it. I am a guest in this country and this is a way I can pay something back."

Recent years have not been kind to royalty in much of the world. In many nations, monarchy is regarded by some people as archaic, or merely ornamental. Nothing more needs to be said about the state of royalty in England, where the crowns have been knocked askew by those wearing them, and the tabloid newspapers have left the poor dears hanging in tattered embarrassment.

Yet, in Thailand, portraits of the King and his Queen, Sirikit, were prominently displayed on the walls of virtually every home and business in the Kingdom. In Thailand, H.M. Bhumibol Adulyadej and his family were revered, in much the way royalty everywhere was, once upon a time. The King of Thailand was—and is—most insist, the embodiment of national unity, the glue that may be what holds the country together.

The glue that held the King together? Surely music played a role. He once told a group of students—who later joined him in a jam session—that "the purpose of music is to educate and relax the mind. We musicians can express our feelings and awaken reactions. Music can be used for satisfaction, for amusement, to help us persevere."

The Name Says It All

Love for Sale

When I arrived in Bangkok in 1993, I was an aging, libido-gone-astray, Western male awash in *The World of Suzie Wong*, Thai style. Welcome to the Land of Smiles, indeed. Thailand had been *the* place for casual, convenient sex for *farangs* since the 1960s and America's war in Vietnam, when the big, pale foreigners came to Thailand for the first time in large numbers for what was euphemized as R&R, and, thirty years later, I joyously joined the parade. Patpong and Soi Cowboy and Nana Plaza were places where nearly anything imaginable was available at an affordable price, where horny males could push "rewind" on life's remote control and return to an unrequited adolescence...and this time, the girls would all say yes and make you think they loved it. I was reminded of something one of the literary McCourt brothers said: "You're never too old to have a happy childhood, and I'm having mine now!" If, as the song promised, "dreams come true in Blue Hawaii," fantasies came true in Bangkok. It was biology at its friendliest, gynecology with a beat.

Some *farangs* told sad stories about the girls they at first claimed to love and subsequently called gold-diggers and worse. In too many cases, the epithets were deserved. Wallets and ATM cards were stolen. Some of the men were drugged as well as robbed. Many bar girls convinced several men simultaneously to send money every month, employing one of numerous commercial services available to answer the letters that came to them, juggling their boyfriends' holidays so that they didn't overlap. (One of the services, located near the American, British and Dutch embassies, was called Language Lovers' Translation Centre.) Money was solicited to pay for fictitious parental illnesses and other needs at home that bore no relationship to reality. Many of the women played their customers along though they already had Thai families. Some even married them just to escape poverty, divorcing them as soon as they were settled in a country where common property had to be shared and alimony—an alien concept in Thailand—was an accepted part of a marital split.

Still others had Thai boyfriends, many of whom took the women to work on their motorbikes and lived off their earnings. More than anyone would suspect actually preferred female companionship. Yet, none of this was revealed as the little darlings crawled all over their customers' laps and whispered, "Number One! Lob you too much! Go hotel?" I had an attorney friend who worked in Phnom Penh and took his holidays in Bangkok who said, "I never knew any group of people who lied more than lawyers until I started spending time in the bars."

Still, the tide of males rolled in, praise going where praise was generally deserved, the thousand-baht notes right behind them. Some of the non-complainers surely were the ones Tennessee Williams was talking about when he said that the city's name said it all. There was no other way of putting it: if you weren't happy at home in Sacramento, Manchester, Frankfurt, or Perth, you booked a flight to Bangkok, where young, beautiful women would give you the time of your life. Even if you were a geek or old or fat and couldn't get or keep it up. Affordably. Paul Theroux wrote that in Bangkok, even the "most diffident" got laid.

But it wasn't just quick and easy sex. Tens of thousands of the pay-bar-go-loom liaisons led to marriage, removing the women at last from the poverty that impelled most of them into the business to begin with. Many actually fell in love with the men, went home with their new husbands, stayed married and became parents. I knew several such couples, in Australia, Europe and the

United States. One of them adopted the woman's son, who subsequently became an avid cricket player. More, including me, remained in Thailand, building homes upcountry for our wives and the new families that usually came with them.

It didn't always work out—how many marriages did?—but it was a nice arrangement, at least initially. And for the women who worked in *farang* bars with no interest in marriage, they kept whatever they got from the men with no questions asked or taxes paid. It wasn't a profession that earned respect for the women— quite the opposite—and too often the exploitation, on both sides, ended in misery. But it was not an altogether bad deal.

No question, sex in Thailand was different from what these men got at home. There, affection didn't come with the lap dance or fleeting (and expensive) assignation. In all countries, prostitution was a service industry, but in the West the emphasis was on the second word; it wasn't just a business, the male often felt as if he were *getting* the business. In Thailand, on the other hand, the emphasis more often was on the first word. Service. With a smile.

Thai women were more compliant than Western women. They weren't secretive about wanting the man's wallet, but most seldom made demands they felt the man couldn't meet. They rarely criticized or complained. They were playful, almost childlike, and however incompatible it seemed considering what they did for a living, they were touchingly (and refreshingly) shy. They didn't mind holding your hand in public, making you look like a stud in front of all the other *farangs* in the hotel and its neighborhood, they laughed at any attempt at humor, and they were superb, intuitive actresses, convincing even the oldest, grossest, fattest and most alcoholic that they were the men they'd been sitting in that grim bar all night longing for. Then did it again the next night and the night after that, some of them for years before marriage, or age, or boredom, or fatigue, or AIDS, or something else retired them.

No one knew how big, or profitable, the business was. Bernard Trink, a longtime American expat who for decades had a half-page column every weekend in the *Bangkok Post* to report on what he called the "demimondaine"—something that never would have been allowed in the more politically correct U.S.—said there were three hundred thousand prostitutes in Thailand. Others said more, or fewer. But whether they were men or women or *katoey* (a term generally used to mean transsexuals or transvestites), there was no question they were numerous, and it was estimated that the "sex industry" contributed between eight and thirteen percent of the country's visitor revenue, depending on which academic or NGO or bureaucrat was doing the wild guessing.

A businessman friend of mine who lived and worked in Asia for more than twenty-five years, all of his business in the travel industry and much of it in Thailand, said he didn't like it that the country had an international reputation of being "a whorehouse with temples." He wished the government would just ban public sex outright, close all the bars and massage parlors and so on, and keep them closed for two years, so everyone could see how much of the nation's economy really was dependent on it. Not just in foreign exchange, but in jobs. Close the bars and other sex venues, he said, and you crippled airlines, hotels, travel agencies, restaurants, taxicabs, tailors and jewelry shops, and uncounted other categories of commerce, putting half a million people out of work in Bangkok alone. Then, my friend said, the government could legalize or decriminalize and regulate the trade responsibly or else maybe get serious about finding some other source of foreign revenue.

Maybe he was right. Thailand used to recognize prostitution as a legal trade. A law designed to fight venereal diseases in 1909 called for the registration of brothels and sex workers, along with mandatory health checks, but otherwise regarded the job without the condemnation that now seems so universal. Then in 1960, sex for sale was outlawed and in 1996 more laws were passed in an attempt to control trafficking, rape and child abuse. By 2003, the government started talking about making it legal again, or at least decriminalizing the trade, the idea being to eliminate the criminal element while opening up new sources of taxation.

It should be noted, by the way, that what my friend was talking about and I was a part of—sex tourism, and all the wonderful and horrible things it led to—comprised the most visible part of the sex industry, but only a small part of it. Although *farangs* and other foreigners frequently were blamed for creating this highly profitable industry, the truth was quite the opposite. Thailand's sex market had been examined numerous times by sociologists, historians and many others, all of whom agreed that prostitution was an integral part of Thai society long before Vietnam, and that most of the sex business then and later was conducted by Thais and for Thais. Numerous international organizations such as the Global Alliance Against Traffic in Women (GAATW) and various UN agencies concentrated their efforts not on the go-go bars and massage parlors and so on that catered to travelers, but on the brothels and other "local" sex venues and trafficking of Thai women overseas (as well as the "importation" of women to Thailand from Burma, China and Cambodia), because that's where the more serious problems were. In the *farang* places in Thailand, the women were there by choice, and even if most venue owners treated the women like cattle, they still were free to come and go.

(Many, if not most, sex workers were given only two or three days off a month, there were no benefits, there was no sick leave, and fines were levied for missed days, lateness, and a host of other minor infractions. Some bars required a minimum number of "bar fines" a month—in the busier places, as many as twenty—and pay was deducted for every one they were short. So, too, with hustled drinks. Although some were promised salaries as high as US$200 a month, double what she might earn in a factory or as a retail clerk, few actually received it. Brothel workers and massage women had it even worse; most got no salary at all, shared their earnings with the boss, and had to pay off the cops. In the bars, that was the owner's responsibility.)

In a book published just after the country's economic crash in 1997, *Night Market: Sexual Cultures and the Thai Economic Miracle*, for my money the only book on the subject on a crowded shelf worth reading, the authors said the boom was "fueled by national and international development polices that deliberately functioned to impoverish certain regions of the country, in order to maintain a heavy flow of age- and gender-specific workers for low-paid unskilled jobs, including those in tourism." This led, they said, to "more desperate families, more and younger women recruited to prostitution and worsening labor conditions, greater competition, smaller incomes, and more menacing health conditions, as safe sex becomes a luxury fewer girls can afford to insist on." I thought this a cynical view, but not entirely off the mark.

In the winter of 2001-2002, a new Minister of the Interior launched a campaign to create a "New Social Order" and dozens, maybe hundreds of entertainment venues (mainly bars) were raided by police looking for underage drinkers and administering piss-in-a-cup drug tests on the spot. [See "Piss in a Cup," page 135.] Few were arrested, but the media invited to go with the cops on the raid dutifully reported how hard at work authorities were at cleaning up Bangkok.

At the same time, Bangkok and a majority of other provinces were zoned and if your business wasn't inside one of the approved "entertainment zones," closing time was moved, for many, from two a.m. to midnight. Dancers were told to put on their clothes and sex shows were shut down, as were a number of clubs. (Oddly, in numerous gay bars, open anal and oral sex continued undeterred.) Forecasts of gloom and doom followed, but I don't think it meant much. It wasn't necessary for a woman to shoot darts at balloons and smoke cigarettes with her you-know-what or disappear beer bottles and live frogs in the same cavities to get a traveler's attention. A bikini on stage and a smile over a cola that cost a couple of dollars afterward was more than most men could find anywhere else.

Whenever I returned to the U.S., inevitably I was asked about AIDS. I always said most of the problem was not in Thailand's tourist bars—although it is there, too—and that government studies showed that more generally it was in places that catered to Thai men, whose promiscuity was as well known as it was rampant. It was a cultural tradition in Thailand for young men to be taken to a brothel by an older friend or relative when they were teenagers as a rite of passage, I said, and it was accepted that they then returned to the brothels for the rest of their lives. Thai law also permitted a man to take a *mia noi*, or "minor wife," and when the leading political party announced in 2004 that it would not allow their party members who were adulterers and polygamists to stand for re-election to Parliament, the protest was so vociferous, the proposed ban was dropped. [See "Shadow Wives," page 81.] Thailand was, like so many "emerging" nations, still up to its hips in chauvinism and testosterone.

It was further shown in studies conducted in 2004 by Assumption University that Thai teens were having sex at a younger age, with one survey claiming that twenty seven percent of those aged thirteen to nineteen had had sexual experiences, and the average age was fifteen. More and more female university students admitted selling themselves by the hour in order to buy cell phones, clothing and other fashion accessories.

This was rarely reported outside Thailand. Instead, international media wrote almost exclusively about foreigners, thus it was the Western customers and pedophiles who got the headlines, not the Thai ones, who outnumbered the *farangs* exponentially. Because the media had clients to satisfy, too, and newspaper readers and TV watchers back home couldn't have cared less about what Thai men did with Thai women, they wanted to hear about the bargirls of Patpong and Nana Plaza and the juveniles. So *they* became the subjects of countless "exposés" and news reports and documentaries and tedious academic tomes, and the hundreds of thousands of sex workers who served Thai truck drivers, fishermen and the military, three of the occupations that drove what surely was one of the nation's biggest service industries, went largely ignored.

Meanwhile, in a quiet little side street not far from several five-star hotels in Bangkok's Sukhumvit district, there was a bar that offered blow jobs starting at ten a.m. A couple of blocks away there was another where the women stood in a line against the wall; those on the left were available for anal sex and those on the right were not, and customers were encouraged to take two in any case; if you ordered a second drink it would not be served, because this was not a bar for drinkers. While in southern Thailand, in an attempt to win back tourists from Malaysia driven away by insurgent violence, open-air restaurants, cafes and go-go bars announced a new policy, allowing male customers to touch any part of the female employees' bodies, including intimate areas, for up to ten minutes for fifty cents.

Shadow Wives

It's probably a good thing that Thai soap operas don't have English subtitles, because if they did, attendance at the Grand Palace and other tourist attractions might fall as visitors remained in their hotel rooms to watch the daily ration of domestic theater. Because however badly plotted and awkwardly acted these dramas may be, they offer a look at Thai society that is closed to outsiders and confirms quickly just how amazing the country can be.

There are numerous unusual aspects of Thai culture and life revealed on these programs—with ghosts and *katoey*, the term used for transvestites and over-the-top homosexuals, just two of the more obvious. Still, the one that intrigues me most and I think would entrance many visitors is Thailand's peculiar take on marriage: the taking of multiple wives.

"What we have in Thailand is legislated monogamy but institutionalized polygamy," Natayada Na Songkhla wrote in *The Nation*. "A man should only have one wife but often ends up with more. People in Thailand are obsessed by the concept of multi-wife households. The fact that we aren't supposed to have them just makes the subject all the more compelling."

This is not to imply that the all men have more than one wife. In a story published in the same newspaper (Feb. 5, 2001), it was claimed by Prof. Nongpa-nga Limsuwan, head of the psychiatry department at Ramathibodi Hospital, that research studies showed that "only one-quarter of Thai male adults keep minor wives." Only twenty five percent? As I write this, I can hear Western jaws hitting the floor.

"Thirty five percent of the Thai men surveyed said they saw nothing wrong with having more than one wife, while fifty five percent longed to have minor wives," the professor said. How many of these might, by some, be termed adulterers and self-styled swingers was not revealed. Nor is the good professor saying Thai polygamists live with more than one wife, as usually is the case in Muslim societies, where the *Koran* (4.3) says, "Marry of the women, who seem good to you, two, three or four," so long as the man can properly care for them. In Thailand, usually there are separate residences. Although *Asiaweek*, in a 1999 story on Thai "concubines," identified a meatball factory owner from Nakhon Patho who said he and his seven wives and twenty children lived under the same roof, this type of arrangement is extremely rare.

As with so many things defining the social order in the Land of Smiles, in affairs of the heart, it pays to be first. Because it is the first wife and the children she bears who get the most respect from society at large and, significantly, all of the man's estate when he dies, unless he has made other agreed upon or secret arrangements. Usually, the *mia noi*, or minor wife (the words translate "little wife"), may have to content herself with stolen evenings and weekends, an apartment or condo, possibly a car, a mobile phone, a reasonable allowance, and whatever gifts and luxuries the man can afford.

Polygamy has been practiced by mankind for thousands of years. Many of the ancient Israelites were polygamous, some having hundreds of wives; King Solomon is said to have had seven hundred wives and three hundred concubines. Up to the seventeeth century, polygamy was practiced and accepted by the Christian church and more recently, the Shakers, Mormons and the Oneida utopian community permitted plural marriages in the United States. And while polygamy is banned by law in all fifty states, *The Salt Lake Tribune* (Apr. 23, 2000) estimates there are thirty thousand such families in the West. And as recently as March, 2004, the U.S. dropped its ban on polygamy as a condition for the resettlement of some fifteen thousand displaced Hmong people, refugees from Thailand. Earlier, male refugees who had several wives were asked to choose only one to accompany them to the U.S..

Polygamy in Thailand was practiced openly hundreds of years ago, when kings, aristocrats, feudal lords, and wealthy merchants kept young, lesser wives as a symbol of their status. Customs changed with time, of course, and in 1935 the concept of marriage licenses was introduced and further multiple marriage was banned. However, almost seventy years later, the practice of taking more than one "wife" remained solidly in place and its illegality was, like many laws in Thailand, almost never enforced, as it continued to be popular with many military strongmen, powerful politicians, and leading businessmen.

Asiaweek (June 6,1997) told a story about Sanoh Thienthong, one of the most influential men in Thai politics—head of one of the largest political factions and for a time an advisor to the current prime minister—when he was the Minister of the Interior in another administration. He was visited unexpectedly in his Government House office by his mistress Jitra Tosaksit, a former beauty queen who had raised three children by the minister. Although she had stayed in the shadows for many years, she was quoted now as saying she now wished some recognition. When Sanoh was told she was in his outer office, he fled the scene.

Other beauty queens and actresses have played the same game. According to *Asiaweek*, Ladawan Wongsriwong, at the time a Member of Parliament, was disturbed by how 'agents' went to ministers with photos of the winners of a beauty pageant in her home district, touting the young women as possible *mia noi*. "Some ministers were very angry" when she brought it to public attention, she said. "The parliamentarian came close to naming philandering colleagues, but settled for listing the minister's initials." One former cabinet minister, found to be "unusually rich" by the National Counter Corruption Commission, in court testimony reported by *The Nation* (May 7, 2003) was said to have "squandered money on gambling and minor wives, prompting his wife to salt away some of his assets in case of divorce."

Is it any wonder the Thai public is enchanted by such goings-on? Or that the "other woman" plays a key role in many television dramas?

How does this work? The answer actually is in the law. In Thailand, there are two kinds of marriage. One calls for a ceremony with a blessing by a Buddhist monk, and the other is officially registered with the government. Although many couples do both, many don't bother to register, settling for the Buddhist ceremony. Thus, the union is sealed with a cherished and honored religious ceremony, and no law is broken because registration isn't required by law. Of course, in many instances, religious rites are also ignored.

Which leads us into the thorny garden of women's rights. Although the situation is changing, and gender equality is enshrined in the 1997 constitution, in Thailand today, as in many other places, women are in many ways regarded as second class citizens, the under-educated and disadvantaged result of an entrenched double standard. There is no law forbidding marital rape and the number of sexual assaults against women has doubled in the past decade; domestic violence is so common, it is rare that police will answer a call. Abortion is illegal except in cases of rape or where the pregnancy endangers the woman's health. Men may claim compensation from any men who had sex with their fiancées, but not vice versa. As is true elsewhere, discrimination in the work place is pervasive: the higher the level, the fewer the women, and women earn less than men in all levels.

In addition, suing for divorce is a flimsy option for Thai women. *Mee choo*, the Thai term for "infidelity," applies only to women, thus for a man to divorce his wife he has only to show a single liaison between his wife and another man, while the male is free to roam without legal consequence; under the Civil Code's regulation for termination of marriage, the woman must prove that her husband not only had sex with another woman but also that he lived with her as her husband. As more and more women, and their supporters, were elected to Parliament, attempts have been made to change the law, but so far there are too many male legislators with *mia noi* or sympathy for those who have them to think any new law is likely soon.

Nor is it clear that all *mia noi* are unhappy. Supatra Ratananakin, speaking for the Friends of Women Foundation, was quoted both in *The Nation* and *Asiaweek* as saying one out of every five counseling sessions she had with women seeking advice on family problems were about husbands taking a minor wife. Nonetheless, she said, "Today's *mia noi* is not always someone who is living with a man just for the money. A lot of minor wives are financially independent women who choose to live with married men because they love and understand one another."

Others are content to be No. 2 because they believe it's better than being No. 0, which is what they were perceived to be, and thought themselves to be, before Mr. Big came along. Studies on the subject are few, but there's general agreement that the minor wife more often than not comes from a social class beneath the husband's, with less education and few if any marketable job skills. In this fashion, becoming a minor wife may be regarded by some as not only a way out, but up.

Venus Envy

After putting on my operating room "scrubs"—a paper garment that came to below my knees and tied in the back, a hat, and mask—I was led into a brightly lit operating room at the spanking-new Bumrungrad Hospital, where a friend of mine, Kelly Lynn Deloito, lay on her back, anaesthetized, covered almost entirely by a leaf-green, cotton sheet. Her arms were supported at her sides as if on a cross (and strapped down to prevent movement), only her manicured nails on show; her legs spread widely and hung in slings at the knees (also belted into place, while still another strap held her waist). Except for her hands and her head, with a plastic pipe fitted into her mouth, to help her with her breathing, all that could be seen was her groin, where a penis lay limp on her abdomen.

Dr. Preecha Tiewtranon briskly entered the room, fresh from a mammoplasty (breast enlargement) in a nearby operating room. He was helped into a clean surgical gown and latex gloves. He called a cheery hello to me and slipped onto a low, stainless steel stool on wheels, rolled into position between the patient's legs, and lifted her genitals to examine them. Seeming satisfied, he sketched a few lines on the flesh on either side of the penis in purple ink and then was handed an electric scalpel, with which he began to cut, initiating what was to be his five-hundred-and-somethingth sex-change operation.

In recent years, Bangkok had become a sort of Mecca for SRS, or "sex reassignment surgery." This fitted the government's campaign to make the city a destination for all types of health care and in the years following the region's 1997 economic collapse, the city's excellent hospitals were aggressively marketed throughout Asia and the Middle East as if they were five-star hotels. Bumrungrad even offered cybernet cafes on several floors, a McDonald's, and a Starbucks, to make everyone feel at home, and the original building was converted into apartments for the patients' families.

I'd met Dr. Preecha several times in his office, with transsexual friends or friends-of-friends, like Kelly, who came to Bangkok to complete their trans-gender metamorphosis. Before moving to Thailand, I'd had a live-in relationship with a transsexual in Hawaii and since then several of her "sisters" called me when they came to Thailand for the final cut.

Dr. Preecha, an Assistant Professor of plastic and reconstructive surgery at Chulalongkorn University, said he didn't know how many of these procedures were performed in Thailand yearly, but said he did one or two a week, on average, with patients coming mainly from Japan, Taiwan, and the U.S., but also from Europe and Australia. Thailand's indigenous *katoey* population—the word is a generic for the cross-gendered and more obviously gay—provided another patient base. The largest density of transsexuals was in Pattaya and, increasingly, in Phuket, where *katoey* cabarets were an entertainment staple. Dr. Preecha said his former students performed SRS in those cities, too.

Most transsexuals—people who actually make physical changes to their bodies, as opposed to transvestites or cross-dressers, who merely dress up convincingly (or not convincingly)—don't have their genitals surgically removed, satisfying themselves with hormone therapy, which tends to discourage body hair growth and adds a layer of fat to cover masculine angularity. They get breast implants, let their nails and hair grow long, and try to learn how to walk and talk and live as women. Some keep their male genitals because they can't afford the surgery, others because they don't want to give up orgasms; many because they don't want to take a step than cannot be reversed.

(Most Japanese transsexuals have their testicles surgically removed rather than take estrogen shots. The effect is the same.)

SRS is a growth industry in the world today. (A funny word to use when talking about what also might be called castration.) Check the Internet and you find surgeons in the United States, England, Sweden, the Netherlands, Belgium, Germany, Singapore, Taiwan and, of course, Thailand. The girls who come to Dr. Preecha say they do so because he has the most detailed and candid web page (he even gives hotel costs and warns of possible medical complications, which many surgeons don't mention) and because of the artistry he's performed on their friends. Kelly, a thirty-six-year-old Hawaiian-Portuguese who was engaged to an engineer, had examined some of Dr. Preecha's earlier work on her "sisters" before making her own commitment. Another compelling factor was the cost—US$5,000 in Thailand as opposed to US$15,000 or more at home.

Thais paid about half what foreigners paid for SRS, as well as for other sex surgery. For example, a foreigner was charged US$2,200 for a mammoplasty, which could be done with either saline or gel implants, and locals were charged about US$1,000. Not long ago in Pattaya some poor *katoey* had condoms filled with a mystery goo inserted into her chest, which of course had to be removed. It was a field where some of the "doctors" were as phony as their surgical handiwork.

The night before taking her final step, I took Kelly and her friend Kalei out for drinks. Kalei had had her sex-change and breasts done by Dr. Preecha in years past and now she was back to have her hips and thighs built up with silicone shots, by another doctor in Bangkok. We went to Casanova, one of the *katoey* bars at Nana Plaza, a three-story congregation of mainly go-go bars in the city's Sukhumvit district.

I'd taken others to the bar before, so when I walked in, the girls gathered around us and removed their tops to show off their breasts while urging Kelly and Kalei to do the same; they didn't mind at all. Some of the girls even dropped their G-strings. More than just a "show-and-tell," this was a hands-on experience as the girls squeezed and fondled each other's implants for elasticity, amid squeals and oohs and ahhs. Pretty soon, Kelly was stripped to her underpants and heels, showing off her silicone hips and thighs, something the local girls rarely can afford.

For an hour, the girls talked about their body parts, swapped police stories and makeup notes, gossiped about where they bought their bathing suits and lingerie, and about which doctors did what to whom.

The next day at the hospital, after having her blood tested for HIV and getting an enema and going through the all the rest of the pre-operative rigmarole, Kelly said soberly, "I know that no matter what we do, we'll never be the gorgeous women we want to be, we'll still be pre-op or post-op transsexuals. But this means I'm doing all that I can do. This is my new birthday."

In the operating room, an anesthetist sat near Kelly's head. Five nurses were in attendance, along with Dr. Preecha's associate, Dr. Sattha Sirithantikorn, formerly one of his students. After making his initial cuts with an electric instrument that simultaneously sliced and cauterized, the lower abdomen was peeled back on both sides of the penis. The testicles were removed, the skin left in place to form the *labia majora* and *minora*, and a hole was cut between the anus and where the testicles had been. The surgeon enlarged the cavity with his gloved fingers. The other physician introduced a stainless steel suction tube to remove the blood.

Dr. Preecha then turned his attention to the penis, skinning it and removing most of the interior and leaving the hollow flap of skin still attached to the body. The end and open side were then sewn to form a kind of sleeve, which then was pushed into the vaginal cavity, an act that gives this procedure its medical name "penile inversion." A ten-centimeter-long object that looked like an oblong egg was slipped into the cavity as the sleeve was sewn into position around it. The "egg" was removed and the doctor inserted his fingers to feel if all was well.

(Dr. Preecha explained that years ago, the skin of the penis was discarded and skin was taken from another part of the body to form the vagina. This technique was abandoned because of scarring where the grafts were taken and because the skin had no elasticity, whereas the skin of the penis was highly stretchable. In some cases, he said, the penis was too short to be practical as a vagina and a second operation was necessary, using a piece of the colon to extend the vagina's length. This was especially true in Asia, where penises were generally shorter than in the West.)

A catheter was pushed into the urethra, so that the patient could urinate during the first days of recovery. The doctor stitched the catheter into place, using the root of the penis and the shortened urethra to form a clitoris. Or, at least, a reasonable facsimile; there was no guarantee it would be sensitive to stimulation. Ninety minutes had passed.

Suddenly, the doctor was up and gone, off to another operating theatre for another mammoplasty, as Dr. Sattha slipped onto the stool to begin the final sewing up, forming the labia. Two small drains were inserted in the labia ridges to take away seepage during the five days that Kelly would remain in the hospital. The vagina was rinsed with a huge syringe of water and a funnel-like instrument was inserted with a condom pulled over the end of it. A surprising length of gauze soaked in antiseptic was then pushed through the funnel and into the condom, filling the cavity, to keep it open and clean. The funnel was removed, the condom was tied off and stitched to the patient's flesh to keep it in place.

Dr. Sattha invited me to examine his and his mentor's handiwork. Did it look like a vagina? There was some swelling and discoloration, natural following any surgical procedure, and the stitches and drains and catheter distracted from the beauty of the surgeons' creation, but, yes, I said, it did. Next, the whole vagina area was packed with gauze that was then taped into place with ten-centimeter-wide adhesive. Now only the catheter and a second tube for blood drainage remained. Kelly was wheeled out and taken to a private room.

The next day, when I visited, she held up a jar of liquid. Inside floated what looked like the neck of a chicken with a penis top and two small eggs. "What do you think?" she asked of her abandoned testicles. "I can get them gold-plated, they'd made nice earrings, yah?"

Five days later she was back in her hotel room, where I found her lying on her back, nude, silicone breasts standing erect like pale oranges, a dildo—a real one this time—inserted into her vagina (with a condom and KY jelly). Following the doctor's orders, she did this several times a day, she said, to keep the cavity open and stretched.

"Look how much I had in there!" she exclaimed as she pulled it out. It looked like six inches (fifteen centimeters). "I'm so happy!"

That night we all went to a cabaret to see the drag queen show to celebrate and two months later, the engineer married the "new woman" in his life.

The Country Club

I met Hans two years ago in a bar in Chiang Mai, where we compared travel notes. After consuming several beers, he asked if I kept track of the women I took to bed with me. I said I hadn't, although I could create a reasonable list, if pressed. I admitted it wouldn't be a long one.

"Do you know how many countries you got laid in?"

"Every one I went to. I traveled a lot with my wife," I said.

He shook his head. "That's not what I mean. You said you're divorced now, right?"

I nodded and ordered more beer.

"So, do you know how many nationalities you fucked?" Hans asked. "You know. Japanese, Korean, German, Egyptian, Thai?"

"Oh," I said, pausing for a moment as I ticked off my modest body count, "—four: American, Thai, Vietnamese, and Indonesian. Five if you count Hawaiian, but she was an American citizen."

He said, "I've fucked seventy-three different nationalities, and this is my first time in northern Thailand, so I expect to add at least one hill tribe girl tonight, or maybe a Burmese. I hear there's a lot of Burmese in Chiang Mai."

Thus I was introduced to a small but what appeared, in time, to be an expanding group of men engaged in a competition to see who could have sex with the most women, not counting in numbers but countries of origin. Men used to count such conquests numerically and with the worldwide explosion of the international travel class—another aspect of globalization—now some of them apparently counted nationalities.

This was quite amazing to me. I'd met many people who collected visa stamps in some sort of geographical quest to see how many countries they could visit. But never had I encountered the same sort of activity determined by having sex in those places. It was, one of the men told me, sort of like collecting stamps. Another, somewhat older dude compared it to the country collecting of ham radio operators.

Initially, I didn't believe it. I thought it was an amusing notion, but I wrote it off to the sort of bragging you find in most bars when men get together and drink. Stamp collectors physically possessed the stamps and shortwave radio fans exchanged QSL cards. How the hell did anyone know who was telling the truth about getting laid? This was, after all, an area of male activity bursting with exaggeration and prevarication. Country club members could point to visa and immigration stamps in their passports, proving they'd been here and there, but what real evidence of sex was truly provable?

"It's done on the honor system," a Brit named Kevin told me in a bar in Bangkok. "That sounds right ridiculous, but it works, because when we catch a bloke in a lie"—and the habitual liar always got caught, he assured me—"word goes out and he can put his stiffy in retirement."

It all sounded like wishful thinking to me. But, still, the notion rang true. For as long as men got laid, I was certain that some of them kept count. In recent times, porn stars and rock musicians and famous athletes admitted to fucking women in the *thousands*. Were the Roman legions or Ghengis Khan or Marco Polo counting?

No one knows how many "members" are in the Country Club today, or even if the club exists. (A few insist it's spelled Cuntry Club, by the way, giving me the shivers of more doubt.) However, it may be assumed that country collecting may be more than a lark, because over ensuing years in Asia from the time I met the first participants back in the mid-1990s, I met others, some of them "specialists" who focused their sexual pursuits in narrowly defined areas. Hans told me he was considering specializing in the hill tribes of Southeast Asia, as that could run the numbers up dramatically. He said Vietnam alone had sixty minority groups.

I also met someone whose activity followed his studies in anthropology, who spoke knowledgeably about Abyssinian Galla girls in East Africa (now Ethiopia) who during the nineteenth century were famous in published anthropological writings for vaginal muscles so skilled they could sit on a man's thighs and induce orgasm without moving any other part of their person. He said his "thing" was to recreate the sexual experiences reported in such classics of sexual literature as the *Kama Sutra* and *Arabian Nights*.

Another member of the club called himself a "sex war correspondent," said he traveled from one disaster area to another in much the same way that the guy who wrote *The World's Most Dangerous Places* tempted his fate. It started in South Africa, he said, and took him to Bosnia, Haiti, Cambodia, East Timor, and Afghanistan.

"You know [Nelson] Rockefeller died in the saddle," he said, "but that was in boring New York. Imagine the final cum in Iraq."

Still another, who told me he was a Hollywood music producer, said he planned to lease anthology rights to songs for a CD he hoped would finance his future travels: David Bowie's "China Girl," Stan Getz and Joao Gilberto's "Girl from Ipanema," the Coasters' "Little Egypt," the Beach Boys' "California Girls," etc.

Of course, history complicates and enlivens matters. As worldwide travel became more convenient and affordable, the score potential of the Country Club ballooned, assisted by recent politics. Not so long ago, a Russian was a Russian (or Soviet citizen); today, she might be Ukrainian, Azerbaijanian, Kazakhstanian or, giving a nod to my friend who likes danger with his sex, Chechnyan.

Similarly, because it's possible to pick up several countries in one location—in Bangkok, for example, there are prostitutes from many nations at work, and in California there are recent immigrants from dozens of nations—another group of collectors, who call themselves purists, insist on scoring in the nation of origin; no migrant whores or boat people allowed.

Actually, I discovered that the guys didn't argue that much about the numbers or criteria. Occasionally, they did quiz each other, trying to find a flaw in the competitor's boast, looking to cut the guy out of the game. But generally I found that the Country Clubbers mainly argued about which nationalities were "best," bickering about preferences for perky Asian breasts and wispy pubic bush vs. the appeal of the hairier, blonder voluptuosity found in, say, Scandinavia.

"It's just good fun, mate," one said in Bangkok. "Did I tell you, I'm writing a book?"

"What're you calling it?"

"Well, first I was gonna call it *Around the World in 80 Lays*, but I decided that was a bit daft. I was in the fifties at the time and wondered what if I got past eighty? Maybe eighty would be common and other blokes would say I was a wimp."

He was silent for a moment as he pulled on his beer. "So what are you calling it?" I asked

"The *United Nations*," he said, proudly.

"I think the name's been taken."

"You're right, mate," he said, "but I mean it. And I figure I'm a piece-keeper. That's a joke. You get it?"

Acquired Tastes

Rotten Fish, Yum Yum!

My dictionary tells me that anything "rotten" is undesirable. It says "rotten" is "foul-smelling, putrid...wretchedly bad; miserable."

That doesn't sound like anything I'd want to put in my mouth. But around the world, many do. And usually it's rotten fish they eat.

I've made a study of the unusual things some people eat in books titled *Strange Foods* (1999) and *Extreme Cuisine* (2004). My message, if I may use such a weighty word, was that what is called weird in one corner of the planet is merely lunch in another. In my research and travel in six continents, I encountered several places where fish was deliberately allowed to rot and then wolfed down with a lot of smacking of the lips, followed by requests for second helpings. For an American raised on meatloaf and mashed potatoes, this seemed very strange, indeed. But interesting. It is my curiosity that's driven my quest, and in the process I've discovered some very tasty dishes.

The locations that got the most credit, or criticism, for putting rotten fish on the menu were in Scandinavia, Iceland and Alaska. In Alaska, the Inupiat and Kobuk tribes traditionally caught what are called *sheefish* with hooks made from bear teeth and buried the catch ungutted in a leaf-lined pit, where it decayed in its own juices for several weeks. It should come as no surprise that the aromatic result was known, colloquially, as "stinkfish."

A similar dish, called *lutefisk* is a specialty of Norway and Sweden. Here, freshwater fish are caught in mountain lakes in August and September, then wrapped in birch bark and buried. The fish remains underground until the first snow, when they are rubbed with salt and sealed in wooden casks for three months and left to rot. When soft enough for a finger to be pressed through without meeting resistance, the fish is soaked and rinsed before steaming or poaching.

The champ in this twisted, gastronomic Olympiad generally is acknowledged to be the Icelandic dish called *hakarl*. This is cured shark meat that is cut into strips and, again, buried in the ground (preferably a gravel bed) for several weeks. Washing and air drying follows—although that doesn't diminish the smell—and it, like all the others, it is best served with whatever local alcohol might be available. In quantity.

What has this got to do with Thailand? Not much, except that when it comes to rotten seafood, the Land of Smiles tops all of them. Here, fermented fish is not a specialty served seasonally or on holidays, it is an essential part of the diet and an indispensable ingredient for its cookery .

I'm talking about *nam pla*. This and its many Southeast Asian variations is made from rotten seafood and is produced by packing small fish—usually anchovies, but sometimes other fish, or even shrimp or squid—into barrels or crocks with salt or brine, and leaving it to ferment for at least a month and for up to a year, after which the liquid is drawn off and matured in sunlight before being bottled. It is then used in the same way salt is used in the West, or soy sauce is added to dishes in China and Japan. Unlike table salt, however, the brown liquid is highly nutritious, rich in protein and B vitamins.

(Crystallized salt is never used as a table condiment in Thailand, but may be added during cooking. Salt also may be added to some fruit juices or used as a dip, with or without sugar and chilis, for green mango, pineapple or other fresh fruit.)

What puts fish sauce into the why-in-the-world-would-any-one-want-to-eat-that? category is its smell. Bruce Cost, author of the excellent survey *Bruce Cost's Asian Ingredients* (1988), likened the taste to "encountering Camembert for the first time. The aroma, fortunately stronger than the taste, is more like an odorous cheese than an aged fish." Others have made far ruder comparisons redolent of outhouses and the you-know-what that's always found in them.

What few realize is that this pungent sauce has been around for a lot longer than Thais. In Classical Greece and Rome, virtually everything was seasoned with what they called *liquamen*, or *garum*, made from anchovies and other fish in much the same manner. Anchovies packed in salt, which lend their dizzying fragrance to numerous Italian dishes, are another inheritance from this kind of ancient fish pickling.

Nowadays, the stuff is found mainly in Southeast Asia, added to numberless dishes during the cooking stage, or after serving, or next to the main dish as the base for a dipping sauce, in Thailand usually combined with chopped chilis, fresh lime, and other ingredients. Variations on the same salty theme are manufactured in Vietnam, where it is called *nu'o'c ma'm*, in Cambodia *tuk trey*, *ngan-pya-ye* in Myanmar, and *patis* in the Philippines. In the United States, usually in shops in a city's Chinatown, I find competition from producers in Vietnam and the Philippines, but everyone agrees that it is Thailand that exports the translucent, brown sauce in the greatest quantity. It probably doesn't have to be said, but fish sauce keeps indefinitely on the shelf, without refrigeration. It's already rotten, so what else could happen to make it worse?

What is not found so widely is *pla ra*, a runny paste created when fish is abused in the same fashion, this time with rice husks thrown in, and the whole sticky mess is eaten, usually using the fingers, with rice. I've been exposed to this quite a lot recently, now that I have a house in Surin, a province in northeastern Thailand where a jar of the stuff is never far from the dinner plate. I confess I have a jar of it in my kitchen in Bangkok as well, its lid screwed on as tight as handcuffs applied by a sadistic cop. Even so, I swear I can see an occasional bubble rise through the glop to the top and when my Thai-Khmer wife Lamyai opens the jar, the "fragrance" fills the kitchen like a hyena's burp, the birds go silent in the neighborhood and geckos fall from my apartment walls. As I watch her dip her fingers into the stuff and lift a smear of it with rice to her lips, I remember that rice and fermented fish were the K-rations that sustained the Vietcong.

Although I think Scott and Kristiaan Inwood, authors of a small but delectable book called *A Taste of Thailand* (1986), overstated the case, I know what they were talking about when they said it recalled the "accumulated stench of putrefying corpses, abandoned kennels, dirty feet, stagnant bilges, and fly-blown offal."

Lamyai calls this blasphemy, says such opinion smells worse than the goopy gray stuff clinging to her fingertips and lips.

Thai Aphrodisiacs: Food That Makes You "Strong"

Before getting into the hard facts, a caveat: what follows was performed at the direction of a magazine's editorial staff; as I told my wife as we ventured forth on each expedition with firm resolve, "Honest, honey, I'm just doing research."

What I learned, in a nutshell, was that Viagra and other pharmaceutical pick-me-ups may have acquired a sizeable following in the Land of Smiles, but there remained a number of gastronomical boosts that defied any challenge from a laboratory in Switzerland, or from all the counterfeit factories in India. At least that was so if you listened to the true believers, most notably the people who captured, cooked and sold the stuff.

Before venturing into one of the countless restaurants that specialize in birds' nest soup—clustered densely in Bangkok's Chinatown and in southern Thailand where many of the nests are "harvested," from the Phang Nga Sea south to Hat Yai—I did a little reading on the subject. This led me to wonder why the first person to climb to the top of a dark, bat-infested sea cave on a rickety bamboo ladder and saw nests made largely of bird saliva, thought this messy bit of housekeeping would make a yummy bowl of soup. Rhino horn, at least, was phallic in shape, more or less, and it wasn't too long a reach to think that a tiger's parts might convey the strength and stamina of what the *Guinness Book of Records* called the most dangerous man-eating animal on earth. Why the nests of birds that, just before their breeding season, fed on gelatinous seaweed that made their salivary glands secrete a glutinous spit, with which they constructed their nests, was added to this aphrodisiacal list may forever remain a mystery.

All that said, on a visit to Hat Yai I happily ordered a bowl and while waiting, talked with the restaurant proprietor. He told me that the dried nests took up to a full day and night to clean, soak, and rinse, and that there were myriad ways of cooking them, but all required the addition of other ingredients—minced chicken and egg white, ham and wine, chrysanthemum petals and lotus seeds, for example, to replace the nutrition totally removed by the cleaning, soaking, and rinsing of the nests. This then was baked inside a coconut or pumpkin, or stuffed inside a chicken and double-boiled, or merely simmered as any other soup.

Although there was a market for dried and packaged nests in Asian groceries and Chinese herbal shops, where it cost upwards of three hundred dollars for about an ounce, making it nearly worth its weight in gold, it sounded like a lot of work and I wasn't surprised when I was told that virtually all birds' nest soup was consumed in a restaurant. However, I was assured, with the customary grin and wink, that the stuff delivered what was promised. So it wasn't a dinner-and-a-movie date, but dinner-and-then-go-back-to-the-hotel-as-quickly-as-possible experience. On the way home, my wife apologized for giggling.

My experience with shark's fin was, sadly, quite similar, and was further tempered by warnings that some species were now threatened with extinction and reports of "finning," the cruel cutting off of the fins and release of the crippled fish to a slow and gruesome death. I also learned that, in much the same manner as the birds' nest, after a long soaking, boiling, and rinsing, the fin was rendered without nutrition and nearly tasteless, contributing only a gooey consistency to the soup. It was chewy and had a pleasing texture, but it was the crab meat, roe, shrimps, sweet-smelling mushrooms and other vegetables, ginger, bamboo shoots, thinly sliced ham, shredded chicken and ginseng that gave the soup its flavor and anything approximating nourishment. Once again, I rushed home with my wife, who after a while said, "Ho hum."

It was time to take a break and review. As I understood it, an aphrodisiac was any substance, animal, vegetable, mineral or, in the modern age, pharmaceutical, that was believed to stimulate a man's or woman's libido, increase sexual energy and performance, and in whatever way possible, enhance the enjoyment of sex. That sounded good to me, but was it reasonable to seek such warming support in food and drink?

Yes, it was true that Aristotle recommended parsnips, artichokes, turnips, asparagus, candied ginger, acorns bruised to powder and drunk in muscatel, that Ovid counseled a mixture of "pepper with the seed of the boiling nettle, and yellow chamomile ground up in old urine," that the fifteenth century work, *The Perfumed Garden* suggested dabbing a paste of honey and ginger directly on the male organ to increase size, and that *The Kama Sutra*, the notorious Hindu guide to love, advised the firmness- or endurance-challenged to boil the testicles of a goat or ram in milk and sugar.

Interesting, yes, but like the birds' nest and shark's fin soup, what a hell of a lot of work, and some of it rather more yucky than I wished.

There was another possibility. What is termed "organotherapy" dated back at least to Roman times, when it was believed that eating a healthy animal's organ might correct some nagging ailment in the corresponding human organ, a belief that continued to the present day. Thus, if eating foods that looked phallic made any sense—to the aforementioned rhino horn add deer antler, sea cucumber, and the geoduck, a clam that can weigh as much as seven kilograms and has a neck like a fire hose, all quite in demand in Asia—it seemed to me that it was time to kick the crusade one level higher—or lower, depending on your point of view—and try a dish or drink whose main ingredient was genitalia.

I confess I wasn't inexperienced. Many years ago I ate the *cojones* of a loser in that day's bullfight in Mexico City (deep-fried), in Singapore I slurped up a bowl of what was said to be turtle penis soup, and in Guangzhou, China, I once drank too much of what the menu described as Five Penis Wine, a liquid of dubious murkiness caused by what I was told were the empowering, powdered genitals of goat, dog, cow, deer and snake. Could I find such an uplifting food or drink in Amazing Thailand? Did I really want to?

It was on a random trip to the Samphran Elephant Ground & Zoo, some thirty kilometers west of Bangkok, that I found what I was looking for. Besides pachyderms, this sprawling, leafy compound also has numerous crocodiles on show. Now, I've never been overly impressed by these large, toothy reptiles in such a setting; they seem little interested in doing anything but soaking their scaly bodies in the cement sided pools or remaining equally motionless on the cement pads, their mouths agape. All that great stuff you see on the National Geographic Channel doesn't happen in captivity.

However, on the way out of the wildlife park, as I passed a display of crocodile skin purses, wallets, shoes and belts, a trade that is permitted by the government for a few breeding farms, I asked if there were any edible products for sale, the clerk brought out some dried croc meat in a cellophane-fronted box, some dark beads that were identified as dried blood (good to relieve pain in the advanced stages of terminal disease, I was assured), and—voila!—what I was told was an adult crocodile's penis.

"Make you strong!" said the clerk, unsurprisingly, telling me I was to grind it up in a mortar and stir the powder into a drink or soup.

My first reaction was disappointment. I found it hard to believe. The crocs I'd just seen lazing in the sun weighed nearly as much as pickup truck and what I was being offered for several thousand baht was about the size of my finger.

When my wife saw what I'd bought, she laughed.

Champagne, black tea, sweetbreads, brains, kidneys, oysters, lobster and crayfish, caviar and roe, starfish, cuttlefish, smoked or salted mullet, anchovies, turtle, prawns, sea urchins, whelks, mussels, moral mushrooms, celery (what's the full stalk look like?), red peppers, wild mint, pimiento, marjoram, parsley, roots of chervil and of fern, radish, lotus, pistachio nuts, cumin, thyme, sage, borage, walnuts, almonds, dates, quinces, musk, caraway, age, vanilla, clove, saffron, the blood of many creatures, dove and pigeon (because of their sensual courtship behavior)...the list goes on and on, and most of these foods are available in Thailand, where some people (people I'm certain are not friends of yours or mine) actually believe that there is priapic power in the consumption of mouse droppings. If even the more mundane in this list delivered what the myth extended, would it be any wonder that so many of us walk around in a constant state of lust?

What was needed in my search, I decided, was something more exotic, a food that would at the very least offer some true gastronomic adventure, without further endangering any of Thailand's many threatened species. Here's some advice from Dr. Schwann Tunhikorn, head of wildlife research for the Royal Forestry Department on the subject of tiger parts: "What people don't realize is that most of the merchandise is fake. I have never seen a real tiger's sexual organ in the market." What is it, then? Dr. Schwann said many were carved from cattle tendon.

My wife and I knew we could do better, so we went to the Klong Toey Market, Bangkok's largest outdoor food market, situated on the edge of the city's largest slum but also within sight of the Stock Exchange of Thailand, so perhaps my purchase here would at least be as promising as buying shares in one of the Kingdom's companies.

Just a few meters from the noisy traffic I met Kui Sai Lim, close to seventy years of age, the last dozen of which he has produced cobra-based tonic drinks and stir-fries. The customer selects a snake from one of several cages nearby, most a meter or more in length, some as thick as a man's wrist and priced according to size, the largest for less than US$20. Enough, we were assured, to provide a healthy, stimulating stir-fry for two.

As my wife and I watched, the serpent was tied to a metal pipe, head up, its tail lashed to the supporting pole below. Mr. Kui then opened the serpent's abdominal cavity with a sharp blade and drained the blood into a glass. A tumbler of strong rice wine was offered as a sort of chaser. The snake—still writhing—was skinned, cut into chunks and filleted, then chopped and cooked with fresh herbs, garlic and chilis.

The last of the cobra cocktail was consumed and that was followed by the usual dash back to my flat and the usual ho-hum and so-what, accompanied by the usual matrimonial smirk.

However unrewarded I may have been in my quest, I assured my wife I would not give up. This was, after all, a reasonable region of research and how could she say otherwise, when tens of thousands, maybe even millions of Asians obviously were better informed and more experienced?

The American writer P.J. O'Roarke insisted that the only sure-fire aphrodisiac was a Mercedes-Benz. Others say there are two, money and power.

I don't even have a motorbike and of the other two, I have none, as well, so please pass the gecko wine.

Gourmet Dining on the Cheap

In the West, street food is severely limited in both variety and imagination. One encounters a soft pretzel served with mustard outside the home of the Liberty Bell in Philadelphia. Roasted chestnuts near London's Big Ben. Tortillas with a filling in Mexico City. A hot dog here, a submarine sandwich there. And most people think "fast food" means you know whose hamburgers, fried chicken and pizza. Or something nuked in a microwave.

Ah, but take your hunger to the streets of the "developing" nations of the world, and especially to Asia, and there you find a level of culinary sophistication unmatched elsewhere. There are no cloth napkins. There are no waiters to take you to the table. There may not even be a table or chairs and if there are, they may be so close to the ground they seem made for small children. But, the food, oh, the food...isn't that what's important, after all, and so often is lost in overpriced, climate-controlled "ambiance"?

On the street, at temporary stalls and rolling carts and from baskets hung from bamboo shoulder poles—here today, gone soon, back again same time tomorrow—is the world's most succulent and tantalizing moveable feast, where diners encounter unparalleled richness and variety, along with a speed in delivery unrivaled by all the efficiency experts behind the international fast food chains. Street food is the original fast food. And not only is the choice greater, it is cheaper and tastier, and also, in most cases, likely healthier.

No one can say which "developing" nation's street cuisine is best, but in any argument, Thailand gets unchallenged respect from everyone. It is for good reason that Thai food has been the most popular cuisine to sweep the world since, well, chop suey and the sushi bar. Visitors to Thailand seeking The Real Thing make a big mistake if they don't eat some of their meals on the street.

Sitting on those tiny stools, knees cracking, struggling with chopsticks, puzzling over why Thais push their food onto a big metal spoon with the back of a fork, while trying to identify the sauces and condiments in the little carry-away rack where there ought to be—and aren't—salt and pepper, ketchup and mustard, can be a daunting, or enlightening, experience. (For the record, the condiments usually are fermented fish sauce, crushed peanuts, dried chili peppers, and sugar, all of which may be added to soup.)

Why, the foreigner may ask, are cold drinks taken away in plastic bags tied off at the top with a rubber band, rather than in a cup? What are all those little pancakes filled with and why is that woman pounding shredded green papaya so mercilessly in a mortar? Are those bananas being boiled in oil? What are those hairy red things piled next to the mangos? Why is so much wrapped in banana leaves or packed into bamboo before it is cooked? Is that toilet tissue being used for paper napkins? Are those insects, heaped high on the tray?

Eating on the street in Thailand is an adventure—noisy, vigorous, and for anyone unfamiliar with the widely ranging Asian diet, sometimes startling. There is no air-conditioned hush that you'd find in most restaurants; a bus and a small pack of motorcycles go past instead. And the food doesn't appear magically from some mysterious location; you watch it being prepared as the smoke and odors wash over you, and if you stand too close to the huge wok full of boiling oil or fat of dubious origin, it will probably stain your clothing. Eating on the street in Thailand is being a part of a show. Gastronomy as street theater.

This is the way food is consumed in Thailand by the local population. It is to the streets and the waterways (where floating kitchens dispense soup and other foods), carts, temporarily erected stalls, bicycles and vendors carrying baskets on their backs, that the rural villagers and urban poor go for a thrifty, nourishing nosh or snack.

Slices of green mango are dipped into a mixture of sugar, salt and crushed or powdered chilis. Iced whole coconuts are "topped" and served with a straw. Beef (okay, maybe water buffalo) and pork and chicken chunks laced onto skewers are grilled over charcoal. Massive ears of corn are grilled in the same fashion, as are eggs and chicken thighs and whole fish (also skewered) and a puzzling array of twisted innards.

Dried, roasted squid on a bicycle rack is run through a set of hand-cranked rollers and reheated over a brazier balanced behind the seat. Lengths of sugar cane are treated to a similar pair of rollers to extract the clear, sweet juice, which is then mixed with water and ice. Sticky rice is cooked with sweet beans in bamboo or banana leaf. A mixture of coconut milk and rice flour, slightly sweetened and slightly salted, is heated in concave indentations in a heavy iron pan over a portable gas burner. The juice of small oranges (never mind the greenish color; they're incredibly sugary) are squeezed as you watch, then poured into plastic bags with crushed ice and tied at the top with a rubber band, the corner of the bag open for inserting a straw.

Crispy-fried grasshoppers, silkworms, crickets, beetles, caterpillars, miniature shrimp, tiny whole frogs and even scorpions are salted and spritzed with vinegar and carried away in small paper bags made from the morning newspaper. Better than popcorn, say Thai gourmands. And lower in cholesterol than many other protein sources, say nutritionists.

As for this being the original "fast food," someday I'd like to see a race staged between a McDonald's serf and a Thai street cook, see who can deliver my lunch first. I'll put my money on the middle-aged woman on Sukhumvit, Soi 4, who produces a healthy bowl of noodles with chicken, bean sprouts, chopped morning glory leaves and stems, garlic and spring onions, a selection of condiments waiting on the table with chopsticks and metal spoons, in about ten seconds flat...and—get this!—nothing had been pre-cooked.

Street hawkers—most but not all are women—are numerous where foot traffic is heaviest—for example, outside rail and bus stations, and along sidewalks where there are clusters of office highrises or, after dark, near the numerous entertainment venues. The food varies from one region of the country to another, but if there is a dominant influence, it is that of Northeastern Thailand, called Isan. Not so many years ago, dishes from this part of the country—the largest, the most densely populated, the poorest—were scorned by outsiders as fit only for peasants. Since then, thousands of food vendors from Isan have set up shop not only in Bangkok but throughout the kingdom and many Isan dishes are now considered a part of the "national" cuisine.

In recent years, there have been arguments about how "clean" Thai street food is, or is not. Pesticides and bacteria have been found in many ingredients. (As they are, too, in five-star hotels; five out of the six times I've been made sick by what I've eaten in Thailand has been after dining at a "nice" restaurant or hotel, not on the street.) The water used by street cooks for washing bowls, plates, and tableware may be of questionable origin. Unlike in the West, few food preparers wear hairnets or hats, or change the oil used for frying as often as they might. The complaints go on and on.

It's all a tempest in a bowl of noodle soup, if you ask me. In a time of mad cow disease and foot-and-mouth and SARS and high cholesterol Big Macs, I find it difficult to get frantic about what I eat on the street in Thailand. The risk is, for me, worth the gastronomical choice and reward.

When I moved to Thailand in 1993, I remembered Edmund G. Love, a long-ago friend in the United States. He was a New York advertising guy back in the 1950s who almost threw his life away with booze, becoming a street person for a while, spending his nights on subway cars. Happily, he sobered up and wrote a book about his experience called *Subways Are for Sleeping*. It became a successful Broadway musical. I met him a few years later when he was researching a follow-up book based on the idea of eating his way from A to Z in the restaurant listings in the Yellow Pages of the Manhattan telephone directory.

Perhaps it was in Ed's memory that when I decided to live in Bangkok, I vowed to try at least one "new" food each week on the street, because I saw so many I wasn't being offered in restaurants, and often couldn't identify. What better way to get to know the country than to consume its vastly varied cuisine.

Ed Love died about the time he got to "M."

I figure it'll be another five years, maybe longer, before I exhaust the possibilities on the street in Bangkok. And then I have all the choices offered in the north and south of the country, where I'm assured there is even more variety.

Country Cookin'

I was traveling in northern Thailand with a group of visitors from Europe, when our van suddenly pulled over to the side of the road. The only Thai in the group, besides the driver, said he'd seen something he wanted to share with us, and as we climbed out of the vehicle, he pointed to some people standing around a small fire in a rice field, about twenty meters from the road.

The fire was of a size you'd expect to see built for warmth in a cold climate. But this was Thailand, so that didn't explain it. Nor did it appear they were cooking, because I couldn't see any firewood, food, utensils, grill or wok—only flames and smoke. Why, I wondered, would a group of what appeared to be rice farmers end a day standing around a small bonfire?

As we watched, one of the men in the group added more dry grass to the flames, and our Thai friend, Yutakit Wanischanond, explained. The farmers were preparing a snack to eat before returning to their homes. The questions remained: what were they cooking, and how?

As the flames died and the ashes fell away, we saw what appeared to be an upturned metal can, large enough to have held about four gallons of cooking oil before it found its present use. One of the men removed the hot can with two sticks, revealing a small chicken and what appeared to be a rack of ribs.

We were being beckoned to join the farmers. As we approached, it all became clear: the chicken and meat had been impaled on lengths of bamboo that were stuck into the ground, then covered with the up-ended metal can, which formed a sort of oven around the meat. After that, dry grass had been piled into a mound, burying the can, and set ablaze. More fuel was added until the meat was cooked.

Gingerly, one of the women with a knife cut away some of the chicken and pork into bite-sized pieces, serving them to us on a piece of banana leaf. One of the men then produced a bottle of hooch, the home-brewed rice whisky called *lao khao*. Some of my fellow travelers objected, saying they couldn't take food from a poor farmer's mouth, but Yutakit explained that refusal would offend. We ate. The pork fell off the bone and disappeared in my mouth as if made of meat-scented air, and from a single glass that was passed around the drink's husky heat prepared my palate for more meat.

Once upon a time, everybody cooked outdoors and every mealtime was a variation of what we now call a barbecue. In the distant times to which I refer, there were no Webers and fancy gas grills. Nor even simple grills. Charcoal hadn't been "invented" yet. There were no pots and pans. Probably it was a while before the notion of a spit was conceived. There was only blazing wood and meat that was tossed casually onto the coals of the fire at the mouth of the cave, turned with a stick once or twice before serving, charred on the outside, still bloody in the middle.

I was a Boy Scout when I was young, so cooking over a wood fire wasn't entirely new to me, though I think my buddies and I got more pleasure from setting fire to things than from eating over- or under-cooked chicken and beef that our moms purchased for the camping trip.

Many years later, I lived in the northern California woods, cooking all meals over a wood-burning stove with a massive metal pipe to take the heat and smoke up and outside the house without, we all prayed, setting it aflame en route. This stove also provided the heat for the house. I recall that after years of cooking over gas in my previous homes, learning to regulate the heat in a wood fire was somewhat dodgy, and precarious.

It wasn't until I moved to Thailand and built a home in a small village in the northeast that I learned how truly wonderful cooking this way could be. Here I was reconnected to the past by my genetic mealtime memory, transported back to pre-industrial times, and to countless millennia earlier, to the basic yet subtle succulence of cooking at its simplest and most eloquent over wood.

In time, wood became increasingly expensive and hard to find in many places, and for a while coal took its place. Coal was easier to store than wood and often easier to get, and it left less ash, but coal fires were as smoky as wood fires and more toxic, releasing dangerous pollutants into the air. Then came gas and electricity and nothing was the same again. If you lived in a modern city in the West, wood and coal fires—for heating as well as cooking—by the mid-1900s were banished in the name of convenience and health. But not so, yet, in much of the world.

Today, cooking over wood remains so pervasive it's blamed for deforestation, as poor villagers roam farther from home to find combustible fuel. Illegal logging and other environmental abuse, together with rampant development, are responsible for much greater loss, of course. No matter how the argument rages, in the foreseeable future for tens of millions of people, wood will remain the kitchen fuel of choice because it is the only affordable one.

In Thailand, and in most "developing" nations today, there are several ways of cooking over a wood fire. One of the most basic involves placing three large rocks (cement building blocks will suffice) in a triangular pattern, building a wood fire in the middle and balancing the metal pan or grill on top of the rocks. Other country cooks own a clay, portable cooker, or brazier, that serves the same purpose, with wood or charcoal set alight beneath a metal grill or metalware placed on top. Many insist that only a charcoal or wood fire can provide the desired heat for certain dishes and keep a small brazier in use long after acquiring a gas or electric stove. In my apartment building in Bangkok, the Thai family next door has one of these on the balcony. Many others are used by vendors cooking food on city streets.

At a recent new year celebration at my home in rural Isan, the men in the family slaughtered and butchered a hundred-kilogram pig, throwing the first slabs of meat directly onto the coals of a large, open wood fire nearby, turning them with a stick, precisely as it was done in prehistoric times. After a few minutes, the hot flesh was retrieved from the coals, sluiced with water to remove the ash, then cut with a machete into bite-sized chunks and served with a chili, garlic, green onion and fish sauce dip.

Meanwhile, the women took other butchered cuts and prepared them over four more wood fires. One was for boiling the pig's feet and head in a large pot, another for grilling, a third for stir-frying bits of pork with fresh-cut vegetables, the last for deep-frying strips of skin and fat. The succulent odor of the cooking flesh blew every which way in the shifting breeze, bubbles of grease so small they were invisible, blending with the smoke in a fashion that made me think, "Hey, capture this scent, bottle it, and sell it as an after-shave!"

The women moved swiftly among us as the various dishes were ready, and we helped ourselves with our fingers and cheap metal spoons. While the men ladled a sweet, milky, home-brewed rice whisky into a cup that was passed from hand to hand.

I asked why the gas stove I'd purchased for the house wasn't being used. Gas was dangerous, my Thai family said; the tank of propane connected umbilically to the stove was, rightly, regarded as a potential bomb. Besides, the women said, they preferred to cook over fuel they knew, trusted and could see.

Thus, wood smoke is now for me and tens of millions more living in Thailand's countryside, the first sizzling scent of the day, as much a part of the dawning as the rooster's cry, an essential prelude to a steaming bowl of rice soup, or grilled chicken, or, during the rainy season when the rice paddies flood, plump frog.

On the Eat-a-Bug Trail in Bangkok

When visiting Thailand, go see the Grand Palace and spend an hour in a longtailed boat touring the river and canals. Visit the Jim Thompson House and take in an evening's ritualistic brutality at one of the city's kickboxing stadiums. Explore a dazzling Buddhist temple or Brahman shrine and be sure to get a traditional Thai massage. And by all means, go shopping.

Then eat some of the people's food: insects.

Admittedly, it's not for everyone. When my daughter, Erin, a first grade teacher in California, visited me in Bangkok and I suggested she try some of the deep-fried crickets, grasshoppers, beetles, silkworm larva and scorpions commonly sold on the street, she said, "Dad, you're more adventurous than I am. I won't eat anything that's cute or disgusting."

She was talking about what the creatures looked like when alive. Dogs and rabbits were cute, so she wouldn't eat them, and insects were disgusting. She was unmoved when I quoted an eighteenth century writer, Jonathan Swift, who said it was "a brave man who first ate an oyster."

"Look," I went on, without result, "you eat lobster and crab, don't you? They're pretty ugly. And when you think about it, chickens are weird looking, too."

The truth is, I told my daughter, who was beginning to wander off to look at the counterfeit designer jeans on offer nearby, insects are eaten in much of the world, and not just as a quirky treat—like the chocolate-covered ants I ate when I was in college—or for lack of money or anything else to eat. In Asia, Africa and Latin America, insects are not merely endured but enjoyed. In parts of southern Africa when the mopane "worms"—caterpillars, really—come into season, the sale of animal meat actually drops.

And, I went on like a professor whose class you wish would end, the cattle industry is destroying the environment. Rain forests are being torn down to create grazing land. Did you know, I asked, that nearly all the soy grown is to feed livestock? And that according to the World Bank, the average cow in Europe was subsidized to the tune of US$2.50 a day? Besides that, insects were higher in protein and lower in fat. United Nations studies in Africa and Mexico showed insects had seventy percent protein, compared to fifteen per cent in steak.

My daughter said, "Um-hum." She now had her eye on some "cool" sunglasses.

That doesn't happen in Thailand, I went on. But of all the places in the world—even in Colombia, where there is a statue of an ant in recognition of its place in the local diet—nowhere outside Thailand were insects prepared and consumed with such year-round regularity and delight. I explained that most of the insects consumed were eaten in the northeastern region, called Isan, and that when residents of this area migrated to Bangkok looking for work they brought their cuisine with them. Yes, I said, it was true that Isan was the poorest region of Thailand, but even when the migrant workers had money in their pockets, they returned faithfully to the insect vendors.

I admitted that there were some insects I had trouble with at first. One was the giant water bug because it looked like a cockroach. Then one day when I met a Thai friend at an outdoor beer bar she had a bag of them. I knew my moment of truth had come.

"Have one," she said. It wasn't a question. So she showed me how to pick off the head and legs and peel away the carapace to get to the abdominal sack which much to my surprise contained a kernel of delight. Not only did it taste good, its fragrance was such that I learned it was routinely pounded in a mortar with garlic and chilis and fish sauce for use as a spicy dip for other foods. I bought a sack and said, "Erin, you've got to try one. You'll really love it. You used to like boiled peanuts when we lived in Hawaii. This tastes sort of like boiled cashews, with a bit of fishy aftertaste. And it smells like flowers."

"Dad," she groaned, "are you trying to make me sick?"

So I let a couple of days pass before taking her to a restaurant called Bane Lao in Bangkok's Sukhumvit district, a place as its name implies where the cuisine of Laos is lovingly prepared and served.

"Oh, look," I said, after we'd been seated, "they have ant egg salad."

My daughter rolled her eyes and laughed. "You don't give up, do you?"

I pointed to another dish on the menu. "Okay," I said, "would you rather have the beef lips?"

I never did get Erin to eat a bug, but I'm happy to report that more and more foreigners appear to be trying them, and it's a darned good thing, too. Because it's the food of the future. As any environmentalist and scientist will attest, the time is fast approaching when cattle, pigs, sheep, and goats—the four leading sources of the world's protein today—will be so cost inefficient as to be unaffordable by anyone except the very wealthy.

Cows consume lots of fodder and water and require much time and effort to produce a single hamburger, whereas insects require little room, don't eat much and breed like crazy. As I explained the food-of-the-future thing to Erin, I assured her the bugs wouldn't show up on her plate looking like grasshoppers and scorpions.

"Think bug burgers," I said, cheerily, without any noticeable effect.

Thai Fire

In Thailand, where restaurants rate their dishes by placing one, two, three and sometimes four little red chilis on the menu next to the dishes' names to alert diners, I am tolerated. Barely. A longtime friend, who is a Thai chef, used to bring home food purchased at street stalls and as she placed it on the table, she pointed to one container and said, "Mine," then to another, saying, "Yours." As if to say, "Poor dear."

Chili peppers are not exclusively Thai, but I can't imagine life in Thailand without them. Thailand cannot claim to be the birthplace of the *Capsicum*—the chili was imported, along with much else in the national diet—it only acts as if it does. Surely, the per capita consumption of the small, fiery fruit is as high or higher than anywhere else.

The truth is, it's an international phenomenon. There's even a bi-monthly magazine published in the United States, *Chile Pepper* (there is no agreement on the spelling), and a wide variety of products is available, including pepper-shaped wind chimes, bells, and strings of Christmas tree lights. There is a Hot Sauce Club of America, where members receive two new hot sauces and a newsletter every month. There's even a popular American rock and roll band that calls itself the Red Hot Chili Peppers. Yes, the band is hot.

Chilis are hot because they contain capsaicin (pronounced cap-SAY-a-sin), an irritant alkaloid found mostly in the interior tissue to which the seeds adhere. (Thus, removing the seeds helps lower the temperature.) Capsaicin has at least five separate chemical components: three delivering an immediate kick to the throat at the back of the palate, two others conveying a slower, longer-lasting, and less fierce heat on the tongue and mid-palate. Mmm-mmmmmm-mmm, say my Thai friends, who have had decades to get used to it.

I still think deliberately eating something that creates discomfort, even extreme pain, is strange. The names of the sauces found primarily in markets in the Southwestern United States say all that needs to be said: "2-Hot 2-Trot Sensual Seasonings," "Inferno," "Tejas Tears Habanero Sauce" ("Hot Enough to Make You Cry"), "Chili Bob's Mean Mother," "Satan's Revenge" and "Mad Dog Liquid Fire."

I mean, why would anyone in his or her right mind want to add that to dinner or lunch?

Actually, some varieties of the *Capsicum frutecens* are quite mild and sweet, but many can only be called hot or fiery. Belonging to the same family as the tomato and the eggplant, they were introduced in Europe by (some say) Christopher Columbus or early Portuguese explorers, originating either in the Caribbean or Brazil. Magellan is credited with taking chili peppers to Africa, the Portuguese with taking them to Asia.

Today, chili peppers play a significant role in many cuisines—from Mexico, where they are used in ragouts and sauces (*moles*), to the Middle East where they are pickled whole, to North Africa where they are used to season couscous with garlic. More chili is added to South Indian curries, while the Chinese make a purée called *ra-yiu* that is mostly oil-based, with fried soya bean and chili as additional incredients. So popular is chili in China that each province has its own brand.

Koreans use a chili paste to make kimchee and hot spicy soup. In Singapore, chili sauce must include garlic and ginger. In Malaysia and Indonesia, it is called *sambal* and often includes shrimp or dried fish. In Thailand, only a short walk from my flat, there are street vendors mixing and selling *som tam*, a five-alarm green papaya salad with lime juice and tomato and as many chopped peppers as you can stand; this dish once was a staple for the poor in Thailand's impoverished northeast, but nowadays it's hard to find a Thai menu anywhere worldwide that doesn't include it.

In Hawaii, "chili peppa water," which is a blend of what it sounds like, is found on every local restaurant table next to the pepper and salt. Throughout the United States chili pepper sauce has a large following, mainly through the sale of Tabasco sauce, manufactured in Louisiana and sold in tiny bottles internationally, and is used to season meat, egg and red kidney bean dishes, sauces and a number of cocktails, including the ever-fashionable Bloody Mary. Not long ago, for a year or so, chili sauce even outsold ketchup in the States.

Just as different ingredients are added to the peppers from place to place, there are widely varying ways of preparing the sauces. Tabasco is fermented in barrels for three years or longer, while in Thailand, the major ingredients—chili, flour and tomato paste—are merely blended together and there is no fermentation involved. Tabasco tastes somewhat sourer and, in fact, is hotter. It's in the use of unprocessed, fresh, ripe chilis where Thailand rings all the loudest bells. Thais also like their sauce free-flowing, where in other countries around the region, the thicker and slower, the better.

Chili peppers should not be confused with pepper, by the way. Pepper, black or white, is produced by grinding the seeds, finely or coarsely, of plants of the specie *Piper*, while chilis are fruits. The chili peppers are the smaller of the two primary types (the other variety is sweet and of no concern here) and they can be green, yellow, orange, red, or black. The smaller the pepper, the hotter it is. In fact, the hottest is the *Capsicum minimum*, indicating that somewhere in the academic realm where plants are given Latin names there was a botanist with a sense of humor. In Thailand, these are commonly called *prik kee noo*, politely translated as "mouse droppings peppers" after their half- to three-quarter-inch length and suggestive shapes. *Noo* being the word for mouse or rat, and *kee* being the word for you know what.

Despite this scornful imagery, chili peppers are now believed to be a possible medical miracle. Not only does the consumption of a single pepper provide a full day's supply of beta-carotene and nearly twice the recommended daily allowance of Vitamin C for an adult, but also that magic ingredient called capsaicin, a compound found in the vegetable that controls pain and makes you feel better. What's that? Makes me feel better?

Consider what happens when you bite into a chili pepper. You think you have Shock and Awe in your mouth, with smart (and dumb) bombs going off from lips to gums to tongue and throat. You're certain that your taste buds have been defoliated. You break into a sweat and reach for your water glass to put out the fire. (A futile exercise, because capsaicin is barely soluble in water. Best thing is to drink milk because casein, one of the proteins in milk, specifically and directly counteracts the effects of capsaicin. Others swear by water mixed with a dash of salt.) Your eyes water and your nasal passages flood. You entertain evil thoughts about the chef and even Christopher Columbus.

At the same time, there may come a strange relief, a beneficial side effect. The messages sent to your brain are similar to those which mark pain and the brain responds to these by stimulating the secretion of extra endorphins, natural opiates that give pleasure. The endorphins then sooth or reduce existing pain not only in the mouth, but also throughout the body.

So far, studies suggest capsaicin reduces pain associated with arthritis, diabetes, muscle and joint problems, cluster headaches and phantom limbs. A study done at the famed Mayo Clinic in the U.S. further suggests that it reduces pain from post-surgical scars. Thus, many people who suffer from chronic pain are now being advised to eat spicy food, either as an alternative or as a supplement to analgesics. It is, then, quite literally, fighting fire with fire.

Chili peppers possess other medicinal advantages. They alleviate symptoms of the common cold by breaking up congestion and keeping the airways clear. (Did you notice that your nose and eyes started running when you broke out in that initial sweat? A capsaicin nose spray is now being considered to relieve headaches and migraines.) Chili peppers also increase your metabolic rate, contributing to the success of a weight-loss program, contain an anti-oxidant that lowers the "bad" cholesterol, and scientists at the famed Max Planck Institute in Germany confirm *Capsicum* can prevent the formation of blood clots by lengthening the time it takes blood to coagulate.

If that isn't enough to convert you—I'm beginning to think about heading for the nearest *som tam* street vendor as soon as I finish writing this—there is growing evidence that chili peppers will get you "high." According to Dr. Paul Rozin, a psychologist at the University of Pennsylvania in the U.S. who has conducted several studies of the chili pepper, the comparison to opiates is not misplaced, although, unlike addictive morphine, a narcotic derived from opium, says "this is a natural and harmless high."

My Thai chef friend, who is reading over my shoulder as I write this, is calling me the Thai equivalent of wimp. She keeps a jar of dried seeds in my kitchen and casually dumps them into soups and onto noodle and rice dishes in a manner that seems suicidal.

"Getting to like chili peppers is like playing with fire," Dr. Rozin said. "Humans tend to put themselves voluntarily in situations which their body tells them to avoid—but humans tend to get pleasures out of these things, such as eating chili peppers or going on roller coaster rides. We are the only species that enjoys such things. No one has ever found an animal that likes to frighten itself."

It's Not Whisky

The first thing you have to know about Thai whisky is that it isn't whisky. When I moved to Thailand and was offered the local brew by Thai friends, I declined—no offense, please—explaining that I'd quit drinking bourbon whisky years earlier because the older I got, its strength went one way and I went the other, so I found it wise to drink something else. Also, when it came to Scotch whisky—sorry, but I always thought it tasted like iodine smelled. I was, I said, a beer and wine person now.

My friends reassured me. They said Thai whisky is not like whisky in the West and, before I could say no, a tot was splashed into a glass over ice and soda water was added with a squeeze of fresh lime. Politely, I took a sip. Hey! It didn't taste like whisky at all. It was mild and sweet and, I discovered as the meal progressed, it also was the perfect drink to accompany the fiery Thai cuisine.

So, if it isn't whisky, what is it? The dictionary says whisky's an alcoholic liquor distilled from the fermented mash of grain, barley for Scotch and in the making of bourbon, maize. Thai whisky—much of it, anyway—is made from sugar cane molasses and rice, or merely molasses, giving it the body and flavor of, well, rum. And those made only with molasses, without any grain at all, *are* rum. No Thai whisky, I learned, was made from rice or any other grain exclusively.

"I don't think the Thais even have a word for 'rum'," said D. Kanchanalakshana, who followed his father into the Thai whisky business and now is the deputy director of production at the company that makes the Kingdom's most popular brand, Mekhong. "Anything brown, they called it 'whisky'. That was true a long time ago when the first western whiskys were imported, and it's true now."

I learned there were other differences, as well. Thai whisky can be aged—something that's done in the West to true whiskys, bettering its value and, most insist, its taste—but it rarely is. Mekhong Superior, available in a limited number of locations, is aged five years, for instance, but the government requires only thirty days. The bottling date can be read on the backside of the label by looking through the glass. Ahhhh! March. That was a very good month!

Young, old...it matters not. Thai whisky is as much a part of Thai culture as *sanuk* and *mai pen rai*. Throughout the Kingdom, no matter what the occasion, and perhaps especially when there is no "occasion" at all, the tall, round and short, flat bottles are brought out, even at Buddhist ordination ceremonies and funerals.

Thanit Thamsukati, a former *Bangkok Post* reporter who now works for the company that makes Mekhong as well as two other "whiskys," Hongthong and Saengsong, began to sing soon after we met. It was a popular Thai ditty about whisky, he said, where the drinker got so happy he fell into the well. A perfect Thai lyric theme, I thought. This was, after all the Land of Smiles. Where I came from, the United States, where whisky's praises are also sung, I don't think anyone ever fell into a well. Usually it was into a depression or a fight or divorce.

No one is certain when alcohol was first consumed in what is now Thailand, but likely it was, as in most places, for centuries a domestic activity. Even today in many villages illegal (untaxed) home brews are fermented and distilled from corn and rice, playing a considerable role in an individual's or village's social life. No northern Thai hill tribe "bride price" paid for the groom, for example, would not include some homegrown brew along with the silver and a hog or two.

Most Thai whisky now is sold under a system of concessions that dates back more than 150 years, when the kingdom created cash-producing monopolies not only in alcoholic spirits, but opium, gambling, and the lottery. (The lottery is still operated by the government.) The most recent concession—currently pumping more than US$440 million into government coffers annually—ended in 1999, and new companies entered the field when the bidding resumed for subsequent contracts, although the usual names prevailed. In recent years, the government's willingness to open the market also saw several privately owned companies emerge. The Saengsong, Chao Praya, V.O., and Black Cat labels, for instance, captured about ten percent of the market.

One of them, Black Cat, initially was known as Maeo Dam, Thai for "black cat," and it sold modestly, then two years ago it was oddly relaunched in its English translation in a television campaign directed at the Thai market. The award-winning commercial told a story—that no foreigner could hope to understand—about a village loan shark. The villager in debt was not making his payments and the godfather wondered how he could afford to drink whisky if he was as impoverished as he claimed. The answer, of course, was Black Cat. The whisky was that cheap!

Not all Thai whisky is drunk by Thais, just most of it. While there are longtime foreign residents living in Thailand who have developed a preference for the light, sweet taste, and a number of visitors give it a try in the same way they order Thai food and a local beer, almost all of the locally produced whisky is drunk by Thais.

The three-dollar-a-liter cost is the main reason. Before the economic bubble burst in 1997, Thailand was the largest market in the world for Johnny Walker black label whisky, one of the world's most expensive and prestigious spirits—and that's in volume, not per capita. But even those impressive sales were dwarfed by the local whiskys, seventy percent of it "white" (colorless) and sold in the rural areas, with caramel coloring added to the remaining thirty percent largely for urban sales.

(All producers boast that virtually all ingredients are locally sourced. Mekhong, for instance, adds a few Chinese herbs and spices to the mix for flavoring—thus qualifying the product for the name "liqueur"—but says that 99.9 percent of the blend is river water, sugar cane molasses and sticky rice. Broken rice is used by some producers because its cheaper and there's more surface to which the mold can attach during fermentation, and sticky rice is used rather than another kind because of its high starch content, which means there'll be more sugar in the finished product.)

There's also more booze for the buck, said Mekhong's Khun Thanit. The alcohol content was lower than in western whiskys, thirty five percent in the colored brew, twenty eight percent in the colorless, versus forty two percent in Scotch, "but if you have to choose between a bottle of Mekhong and four small beers that'll cost about the same, you go for the whisky." It's more social, too. Traditionally, one person buys the whisky and shares it with friends, and a bottle can last all evening or afternooon. Four beers are bought individually, thus the bonding ritual is gone and so is the beer, in twenty minutes.

"*Chok dee krup* (or *kaa*)!" is the standard toast, meaning good luck. And the whisky is always sipped. Good whisky is never, ever gulped, even when it's rum.

Life is Cheap, *Mai Pen Rai*

Piss in a Cup

My thirty-year-old son was visiting from the United States. It was Friday night and we planned to leave Bangkok in the morning by train to go to the rice-growing village near the Cambodian border where I was to be married on Monday. My son, Nick, is a Mormon, so he doesn't drink, but I had some business to do with the owner of the Q Bar, one of the city's most popular upscale nightclubs, so that was our evening destination.

Nick drank a Coke and I had a Heineken and it was about ten o'clock when we decided to leave. I opened the door and there, to my great surprise, stood a wall of Bangkok cops. I thought that there'd been a fight or perhaps even a shooting outside that we hadn't heard. I excused myself politely and made to walk around the boys in brown and the officer nearest to me held up his hand in a manner that made it clear I wasn't leaving. It was then that I noticed a table had been set up nearby and that on it were some paper cups.

"Uh, Nick," I said, "you're about to be told to piss in a cup. It's part of the country's anti-drug campaign. Everybody in the bar will now be tested for drugs. The cops will take us, one at a time, into the toilet and watch us as we give them a urine sample. They will then pour it into that flask of blue liquid on the table and if it turns purple, we're going to miss the train."

This sort of thing had been going on for some time as a part of the new prime minister's crusade to make Thailand drug-free, a key part of what he called his "New Social Order." Cops had been raiding bars for several months, conducting on-the-spot tests for two of the city's favored drugs, amphetamines—called *yaa baa*, or "crazy medicine"—and ecstasy. Arrests had been few, but the inconvenience to the bars and their customers had been enormous; if the place had a good crowd, as the Q Bar did on weekends, it might be dawn before the last patron was released. I was glad we were first in line.

Nick and I did as we were told and then watched a cop pour the samples one at a time into the flask and stir it around. The color didn't change and we were told we could depart. We stood around for a few minutes to watch. The cop emptied the flask following each test, poured in more of the blue liquid without any attempt to clean the flask, added the next poor soul's urine, and swirled it around with the same swizzle stick that he'd used in ours. What if we'd tested positive? (A reaction that was known to be caused by numerous legal pharmaceuticals, such as anti-histamines.) Would the same unwashed flask and stirrer continue to be used, and contaminate the next sample?

It wasn't a question that I felt compelled to ask and we walked home and the next morning we made our scheduled eight-hour train ride upcountry and on Monday, the first day of January, 2003, I was married.

Exactly one month later, the prime minister got serious and took his "War on Drugs" nationwide, promising a country the size of France with a population of more than sixty million that it would be completely drug-free in three months. (Don't laugh. The same guy once said he'd end Bangkok's traffic problems in six months. He was serving in another prime minister's cabinet, five years earlier.) Lists of suspected drug users and dealers were compiled in every province at the Interior Minister's order. Provincial governors and police were told that those who failed to eliminate a prescribed percentage of the names from their blacklists would be fired. In two months, the body count surpassed two thousand and the newspapers were accusing the cops of "extra-judicial killings."

The police denied the charge and said the dealers were killing each other in battles over territory and to eliminate people who might snitch to the cops. The Interior Minister said that he didn't like the use of the word "killed," asking media to say "expired." After that, the government continued to announce figures for suspects arrested—a figure reported to be over ninety thousand—but stopped releasing the number of deaths. At the end of the ninety days, when the Prime Minister declared his mission accomplished and now reported a body count of 1,612, the actual number was thought to be more than two thousand three hundred. By year's end, the official number of dead dropped to 1,320, only fifty-seven of them reportedly killed by police.

The U.S. State Department, Amnesty International, the United Nations, national and international NGOs criticized Thailand harshly and in the first report by Thailand's own National Human Rights Commission, created by a progressive new constitution, lamented what it called (quoting *The Nation* of August 6, 2004) "the drastic deterioration of civil liberties and the ever-growing, intertwined powers of the state and groups with vested interests." The government was accused of fomenting a "culture of authoritarianism," saying it had "committed gross human rights violations, particularly with its brutal war on drugs, in its quest to promote state power."

The government's response was to blame the commission for its "disservice" to the country, saying that its report had (now quoting Kavi Chongkittavorn, *The Nation's* editor, August 9) "undermined the country's international standing." As for all those killed in the War on Drugs, the government ordered the police to conduct an investigation, giving them a month deadline. A year later, no report had been submitted.

Drugs have played a major role in Thailand's history and its government. For centuries, the monarchy held a monopoly on the sale of opium (along with gambling, alcohol, and a national lottery) and not until 1954 was the residue of the poppy plant and its byproduct heroin outlawed, by which time the police themselves figured prominently in the trade. As chronicled in

David K. Wyatt's authoritative *Thailand: A Short History* (1984) and quoting a columnist who wrote under the name Chang Noi in The *Nation* (Jan. 20, 2003), the Golden Triangle was developing into the world's primary area of production when the chief of the national police, General Phao Siriyanon, used his men to "move the goods from the Triangle to the world market. Police escorts met the convoys at the Burmese border and took them to Chiang Mai or Lampang. From there the goods traveled to Bangkok by train or plane. The marine police then guarded their transfer to freighters in the Gulf.

"In 1955 the police made a record capture of twenty [metric] tons of opium, and Phao himself collected a massive reward on behalf of an informer. When asked to display the haul, Phao said it had been thrown in the sea. The public disbelief almost undid him. On another occasion, a seized cache of high-grade opium turned out to be low-grade mud."

It wasn't until the 1990s—with the infusion of tens of millions of dollars from the United States, police and army raids on opium farms in the north coordinated by the U.S. Drug Enforcement Agency, and a royally supported crop substitution program—that the plant was marginalized as a source of income for mainly hill tribe minorities who had used opium for millennia not only as a cash crop but as their primary medicine.

About the same time, amphetamines swept across Thailand like a monsoon rain, quickly becoming the national buzz of choice. Simply and cheaply produced primarily in China and Burma, it found a market in Thailand that ranged from poor truck drivers and construction workers to rich university students. This was followed by ecstacy and, to a lesser degree, cocaine and LSD and ketamine, the last one easily manufactured, with ingredients purchased at the neighborhood pharmacy, by anyone with access to a microwave oven. This is what led to Thailand's "piss in a cup" campaign.

According to Father Joe Maier, an American Catholic priest who worked with the poor in the Bangkok slums for more than thirty years, the War on Drugs was a complete and utter failure.

All it did, he said, was make the dealers smarter and quadruple the price of *yaa baa*, which drove those who could no longer afford it to seek other chemical highs—among them smoking powdered Tylenol and mosquito coil. Father Joe, whose Human Development Foundation administers Bangkok's most modern AIDS hospice, also points to the damage done by the government's refusal to introduce a needle exchange program for intravenous drug users, many of whom end up in his and the government's care.

Marijuana, generally known in Thailand by its Hindi term, *ganja*, has a more benign history, although it was from the 1960s onwards a cash crop grown by the Thai "mafia" for export largely to Europe and North America; one of the favored smokes in the U.S. at that time was a stem of sticky flowers and buds, tightly tied around a sliver of bamboo and called Thai Stick. It was also commonly grown as an herb used in household and commercial cooking, along with basil, chilis and lemongrass, especially in Thailand's rural eastern seaboard and poor northeast. Long after its cultivation and sale were made illegal, if you were a known customer in many small restaurants, you could have it added to your curry or soup at no extra cost.

Although such open use was curtailed and traffic of all illegal drugs was driven further underground by 2004, drug use continued in much the same way it did in hundreds of countries around the world, most remarkably in the United States, the world's largest market. With the *yaa baa* factories getting support from the Myanmar (Burma) government and huge profits to be made either selling the stuff in Thailand or moving it through the Land of Smiles for export elsewhere. Although millions of pills were confiscated and more alleged dealers were shot while resisting arrest, and over sixty percent of court cases involved drugs, the traffic seemed little affected.

How did the average, non-drug using Thai citizen feel about all this? *Mai pen* rai seemed to be the phrase of the day: never mind, the recently deceased and those incarcerated in jails—built to hold about ninety thousand (now housing over two hundred and fifty thousand)—were a scourge, and Thailand was improved by their removal from the streets or life. NGOs, academics, and some of the media continued to grumble about the damage to human rights and the justice system, but few others seemed much to care.

At the same time, with the royal family's financial support, a five thousand-six hundred-square-meter museum called the Hall of Opium opened in Golden Triangle Park in Chiang Saen, where the Mekong River separates Thailand from Laos and Myanmar. The aim, quoting the museum brochure, was "to further educate the public at large on the serious effects narcotics pose to the national economy and society as well as to the people's physical and mental well-being."

What once had been considered medicinal, or recreational, and a cash crop for an ethnic minority, was now simultaneously regarded as a threat to the nation's health and, according to the *Bangkok Post*, "a world-class [tourist] attraction."

Violence

Thais are non-confrontational, they are a people of accommodation, gentleness and peace. Thailand is the Land of Smiles, a place of harmony and courtesy where showing anger is a major taboo and the cool heart (*jai yen*) is sought and praised. Thailand is where no matter what happens, you say, "*Mai pen rai.*" Never mind. *Que sera, sera.* Water off my back. And get on with your life.

Buddhism says you can't so much as kill a fly; Buddhists will not work in the abattoirs slaughtering pigs and water buffalo for the family table. Unlike other "religions," throughout its peaceful march of two thousand five hundred years, blood has not been shed in the name of the Buddha. Ninety percent of the Thai population is Buddhist.

So why is there so much violence?

Why is there so much cruelty and savagery in Thailand's history? In what is the country's most popular film, *Suriyothai*, generally agreed to be an accurate depiction of Thailand's early royal dynasties, numerous enemies were decapitated and a child-king was beaten to death with a sandalwood club after being placed in a cloth bag so that the executioner's weapon would not make contact with royal flesh. Why is there this legacy of brutality?

Why, more than a dozen years after the uprising of 1992, is Thailand still puzzling over the deaths of students who were shot in street protests, still demanding the names of those responsible, and an explanation for what happened to the many still "missing"?

Why are rape and domestic violence and pedophilia and other forms of abuse of women and children so rampant at all levels of Thai society? (According to a survey by the United Nations Development Fund for Women, forty four percent of Thai women had experienced physical and sexual assaults by their spouses and, in 2003, the Thailand Research Fund said forty six percent of children were attacked verbally and physically.)

Why is the national sport, Muay Thai—kickboxing as it's known in the west—a part of every Thai male's military training, and as one of the world's most brutal forms of one-on-one combat, responsible for so many fatalities? At least one a week, according to one authority.

Why do so many of the trade and technical schools have rivalries that turn into gang-like "wars" that result in students getting killed?

Why do so many young men kill themselves racing motorcycles on public streets?

Why do so many Thais enjoy chicken fights and battles between fighting kites and bulls and beetles and Siamese fish?

Why do magazines and newspapers publish so many gruesome photographs of corpses, and why is the most popular ghost in movies a woman's head flying through dark woods, trailing intestines?

Why are so many business disagreements resolved when one party hires a gunman?

Why are so many canvassers and other political workers and community leaders killed during the run-up to an election?

Why, from 2001 and 2004, were sixteen environmental activists murdered for opposing what they considered uncaring development by prominent politicians and businessmen? (All the cases remain unresolved.)

Why are extra-judicial killings matter-of-factly accepted as a part of the Thai way of life (and death)?

In 1996, six suspected drug dealers were executed while in

police custody in Suphan Buri minutes after they had surrendered in front of television cameramen and photographers. The men were then taken back into the house where they'd held some hostages (who had been freed before the six surrendered), gunshots were heard, and when the police emerged, they said the men were killed in self-defense.

This wasn't an isolated case. According to statistics from the Ministry of the Interior, ninety cases of extra-judicial killings were reported in 1995; forty-eight in 1996; sixty-eight in 1997; and forty-seven in 1998. Three years later, in *The Nation* (July 25, 2001), a front page story was headlined, "Police Death Squads Run Riot." What followed sounded like I'd gone to sleep the night before in Bangkok and awakened in the morning in Bogota or Baghdad.

"Police-backed death squads are executing suspected drug traffickers in the lower Northeast," the story began, naming the part of Thailand where I have a house and family, "and intend to kill as many as one thousand people this year, the region's police chief said yesterday." The Region 4 chief, Lt. Gen. Pichai Sunthornsajjabul, was then quoted as saying, "Our target is to send one thousand traffickers to hell this year, to join some 350 before them." Sure enough, in a program called "Shortcut to Hell," three men suspected of dealing amphetamines were found dead a few kilometers from my house a few weeks later.

The chief explained that an anti-drug "alliance" comprising police, soldiers, government officials, civilians, and members of "private organizations" had been working as an intelligence-gathering arm of the regional police. Once the alliance's tips were confirmed, he said, police would consider whether there was enough evidence to prosecute.

"If there's not enough evidence to take legal action [but we are sure they are involved in the drug trade]," *The Nation* quoted the Lieutenant General as saying, "drastic measures will be taken by members of the alliance. We have applied legal means, political science and even Buddhism, but the [drug] problem only seems to be getting worse. Now it's time to rely on [the]

Death Angel. Of course, it's a legally delicate means, but it's the path we have to take to bring peace back to society."

There were some twenty million people under his jurisdiction, he concluded, and "if a thousand social troublemakers go missing, I don't think it will cause anyone any problem."

The next day, Pichai denied that summary executions were occurring under his jurisdiction, or that he condoned such a practice. He blamed the deaths on armed vigilantes. *The Nation* stood by its story and, soon after, the *Bangkok Post* quoted a commander attached to the Muang Loei district police station (in the northeast, near the Laos border) as saying his men had killed sixty six suspected drug traders who resisted arrest between January and September (2001). Another eleven were reported missing.

In 2003, the prime minister declared a nationwide "War on Drugs." Ninety days later, an estimated two thousand five hundred suspected drug dealers and abusers were shot dead. [See "Piss in a Cup," page 135.] A year later, in what appeared to be separatist incidents in Thailand's southern provinces, another five hundred were killed.

Every country has its bad cop stories and incidents of ugly violence. My own country of origin, the United States, surely is one of the most brutish and homicidal in recent history (dating from the 1700s). But no one ever said America was a peace-mongering nation. The U.S. is the biggest bully on the block nowadays and it seldom lets the world forget that, sending its peacekeeping missions and unilateral war-making troops wherever it decides, even when the United Nations calls its actions illegal. It's also the world's number one exporter of weaponry, has the highest per capita ownership of handguns, refuses to sign the nuclear proliferation and international land mine treaties, has the world's largest military defense budget, etc., etc., etc.

Thailand, on the other hand, is known for its social and cultural restraints on direct confrontation. And with good reason. Because it is non-threatening, most of the time. I think most people agree that Bangkok may be one of the few major cities in the world where it is reasonable to say that no matter where you are, or when, you are comparatively safe. At least from muggings and the sort of street crime so common elsewhere that it doesn't even make the morning papers.

But there's this high incidence of and fascination with violence in Thailand. Why?

Kanjana Spindler, assistant editor, editorial pages, wrote in her weekly Commentary in the *Bangkok Post* (February 19, 2003), "The question comes to mind of just how violent a society we are. After all, we claim to be a predominantly Buddhist nation and if most people claim to subscribe to Buddhism's basic tenets then we shouldn't tolerate violence against one another at any cost. In reality, of course, we are probably much less Buddhist than we might like to claim."

Dr. Kriengsak Charoenwongsak, the executive director of the Institute for Future Studies for Development, a regular contributor to the *Bangkok Post*, believes much of the popular manifestations of violence, such as Muay Thai, "is catharsistic: it allows people to vicariously satisfy their inner drives to succeed at any cost including untempered aggression. Instead of fostering feelings of pity on those weaker than ourselves, boxing is the practice of finding satisfaction in seeing the opposition being completely crushed, something one cannot do in real life because it is against moral standards and the law. Subconsciously, people who like boxing accept the idea that hurting other people is normal."

William J. Klausner, a former professor of law and anthropology at Thammasat and Chulalongkorn Universities and an ex-editor of the annual publication of the Buddhist Association of Thailand, agrees. In *Reflections on Thai Culture*, published by The Siam Society (1981), he said that to fully understand the Thai personality, "we must appreciate that the 'cool heart' and the ubiquitous smile are quite often merely cultural masks covering emotional concerns related to dignity, face, perceived status. There is strain and tension; and release is sought, at least initially, through indirect methods. When these techniques are no longer psychologically satisfying or effective, extreme forces of violence may well result."

Which makes Thailand sound like just about everywhere else on earth.

The Hustlers

One of the things I enjoy most about the *Lonely Planet* guides to any traveler destination is the section that appears early in the book about what it calls, almost whimsically, "Dangers & Annoyances." This is the list of warnings given in an introductory section called "Facts for the Visitor" better known for its advice about "When to Go...What to Bring...Holidays & Festivals...and Things to Buy."

"Although Thailand is in no way a dangerous country to visit," the section begins in a recent edition, "it's wise to be a little cautious..." Indeed. There follow warnings about women traveling alone, guests leaving valuables in hotel safes, credit card fraud, drugs and druggings, assault, insurgent activity and the violent Malay-Muslim movement in Thailand's south...and in the nearby pages on "Health," there are further cautions about everything from sunburn, prickly heat, and snakes to dysentery, cholera, viral gastroenteritis, hepatitis, typhoid, worms, schistosomiasis, rabies, TB, diptheria, bilharzia, malaria, dengue fever, Japanese encephalitis, bedbugs and lice, leeches and ticks, and a supermarket of STDs and HIV/AIDS

One wonders why anyone gets on a plane.

Yet, for me, the biggest bummer are the touts and the scams. It doesn't matter if the visitor is a backpacker staying in a five-dollar-a-night guesthouse or a businessman lodging in a five-star hotel, there are hard dollars and euros and yen to be spent and dozens of Thais lined up to take them, sometimes by any means possible. "Thais are generally so friendlly and laid-back," *Lonely Planet* says, "that some visitors are lulled into a false sense of security that makes them especially vulnerable…"

"I've been coming to Bangkok for more than twenty-five years," a friend who stays at one of those high-end riverside hotels told me, "and I have to say, it's not as bad as India yet, but the way I'm bothered on the street by people who want to sell me something, for sure that that's the way this country's going. I bet I was approached twenty-five times today. It's going to kill tourism, eventually."

He's right, of course, at least about the more aggressive hustlers, con artists and vendors. It might be mentioned that my friend's quarter century in Asia was spent in the travel industry, so I think he knows what he's talking about.

Whenever I travel, I miss Bangkok and I'm always glad to be "home" again, but I dread the journey's end: getting from the airport to my flat. If I forget to give the driver my destination in Thai, chances are about fifty-fifty that he'll try some kind of con: "forget" to turn on the meter or say it's broken, fail to give me my change when passing through an expressway toll booth, or take the long way round to keep the meter running.

It's worse, as my friend said, on the street. How many visitors are scammed by tuk-tuk and taxi drivers and freelancers on foot into visiting a jewelry shop owned by an "uncle" or a "cousin" who has a special sale going; others are told a new government tax will increase the price in just two days, etc. This happens with such frequency—and the gems and jewelry always turn out to be worth far less than what the sucker pays—a government office has been established to handle the complaints.

Imtiaz Muqbil, a travel columnist for the *Bangkok Post*, wrote (June, 2002) that tourism officials admitted that "cheating and fraud is the biggest source of complaints they get internally. Jewelry shops overcharge visitors by several times the actual amount, mostly in order to pay the hefty commissions given to guides, tour bus drivers and the owners or managers of tour operating companies.

"Shopkeepers generally know they have that one chance to squeeze visitors; a tourist is not generally considered a repeat customer. Even though they blame themselves for not having been more careful, they exact revenge by going back home and spreading the word among friends and colleagues."

What my friend was talking about is worse. It's not just a tired old con that includes telling the tourist over-valued gems that will kill the golden goose, but the constant hassle of walking along a shopping street, where vendors—whose stalls already occupy most of what should be pedestrian space—beckon and call and hold out their hands as if to say hello; the automatic response is to shake hands, but then try to get yours back. Making eye contact or glancing at the goods brings the vendor to your neck like a hawk.

Patpong at night may be the worst. Many visitors go there exclusively for the night market, but that doesn't deter the touts who stand outside the sex venues. "Come inside! No cover charge! Take a look!" they cry. And if you're a single male or in a group of males, touts hold up brochures for massage parlors or merely whisper, "Want lady? Want man? Want boy?" While others hold up signs announcing 'PUSSY PING-PONG SHOW, PUSSY CIGARETTE SHOW, PUSSY COLA SHOW..." Numerous bars in Patpong and elsewhere also station women outside whose job it is to physically pull and push men toward the doors.

I'm not without compassion. I've lived in Thailand long enough to know that the touts and cabbies and street merchants are extraordinarily poor. One of my closest friends is an American Catholic priest who has lived and worked in the slums for more than thirty years and I'm down there nearly every week with him, so I know how many of these people live, and how precarious their survival may be.

I still don't like being pestered and hustled, and I don't think anyone else does, either. Thailand seems to be growing ravenous in its attempt to pull more and more money from its visitors, in ways that seem not just larcenous, but mean-spirited. National parks and numerous privately operated tourist attractions now have a double tier system where foreigners sometimes pay several hundred percent more to enter than someone with a Thai face. Dress codes for some of the most popular visitor destinations—the Grand Palace, for one—require foreigners to wear sandals that cover the heel—"approved" sandals are for rent in a shop nearby—while Thais may enter wearing any sort of footwear or none. (The barefoot Buddha, an Indian by birth, would have been turned away.) Until Summer 2002, a foreigner's mobile phone wouldn't work in Thailand, part of the fallout from the monopoly that controlled the industry, a concession held, incidentally, by the man who is now the prime minister. Many laws are enforced only for visitors, police usually accepting a small contribution, for instance, instead of the full two-thousand-baht fine for littering. When shopping on the street, a foreign face automatically doubles or triples the price.

It is as if every form of banditry is directed against foreigners, not just by the greediest of freebooters who probably think of themselves as entrepreneurs, but also by the authorities. For a time, many visitors from China—Thailand's fastest growing source of tourists—were being taken such advantage of, the Chinese government threatened to put Thailand on a don't-go-there list for its citizens unless the independent package tour business was cleaned up.

That put some agencies out of business, but complaints generally go nowhere. "The Thai police are usually of no help whatsoever, believing that merchants are entitled to whatever price they can get," said *Lonely Planet*. "The main victimizers are a handful of shops who get protection from certain high-rankling government officials. These officials put pressure on police not to prosecute or to take as little action as possible."

The foreigners are not totally blameless. Most shoppers buying designer gear and computer software and other counterfeit goods at flea market prices know the stuff is bogus, so they have no legitimate complaint when the forty-dollar Rolex watch stops ticking as soon as the plane takes off for home. While many gem buyers, motivated by personal greed, choose to believe the lie that the stuff will have greater resale value back home.

Still, for more than a decade, tourism has been one of Thailand's main revenue sources and since the financial collapse of 1997, many officials have come to regard its expansion as the economy's savior, rather than institute the reforms that might fix some of the problems that led to the crash.

Change sometimes comes to Thailand as slowly as it can come rapidly, depending on what's to be altered and who benefits. Because they're so rampant, and pervasive, dishonesty and fraud will not be easy to tackle. "Yet," wrote Imtiaz Muqbil, "it could have a more devastating impact on the country's image because it flies directly in the face of tourist propaganda which generically presents Thai people as being friendly, hospitable and good-natured.

"Having thus been lulled into a sense of complacency, visitors find themselves doubly shocked, annoyed and frustrated; they feel cheated by the incident itself as well as by the official literature which sought to convince them otherwise."

The Bodysnatchers of Bangkok

The sounds of windscreens shattering, car parts crumpling, skulls bursting, guns banging away, screams sailing into the night are still echoing when the city's bodysnatchers arrive. These are the Buddhist "rescue" crews who scrape up victims of violence on many of Thailand's city streets, helping the police identify the still warm deceased, arranging and paying for final rites and cremation if no one claims the corpse. The Buddhists believe they make merit this way.

Call it instant karma.

Most modern cities elsewhere have public ambulance services. In Bangkok, and in other Thai cities, where only a few private hospitals have such modern conveyances, a number of Buddhist foundations take up the considerable slack. In Bangkok, the largest and oldest, Poh Teck Tung, is located in Chinatown. For eighty years, this outfit has kept its vehicles on the road, using pickup trucks to transport the bodies to a hospital or the morgue until they were replaced a few years ago by air conditioned vans equipped with sirens and flasher lights.

The second largest and oldest is Ruam Katanyoo, which is more Thai than Chinese in its membership and until 1995, its members competed for bodies with Poh Teck Tung, the rival teams sometimes getting into fist-fights over who got the corpses and the merit that came with the higher body count. Finally, the city government divided the metropolitan area into zones and gave the foundations schedules whereby they'd alternate coverage so no one would miss a regular turn in the most active areas.

My plan was to spend a night with Poh Teck Tung with a photographer for an English magazine. Our driver—wearing a mustard-colored jump suit covered with Thai and Chinese lettering—explained the routine. The crews worked eleven-hour shifts, six days a week, and waited for calls at assigned locations, usually petrol stations where there were convenience stores for buying coffee and snacks. There, they monitored their police radios and sped off to any crime scene or accident in their zone, often arriving before police. Victims were taken to the nearest hospital, dead or alive—the deceased to be collected at the end of the shift and transported to the city morgue. They were called "rescue" teams, but they only received five days of paramedic training and there wasn't so much as a first aid kit in the van. Meat wagons was more like it; in Thailand, better than no wagon at all.

Some said the workers took the job not for the excitement or karma but the riches. There have been reports of money and jewelery "lost" while traveling. The foundations deny this. After all, wouldn't that wipe out the good karma?

The first night we sat in the petrol station for eight hours without a call. We started at seven and by midnight, we were listening to a radio phone-in show for that part of the Thai population—puzzling in its size—that enjoys gore. In the absence of any real violence, we listened to other people describe their favorite accidents, those they had witnessed or their own.

At two a.m., I bought a beer, thinking that might trigger an accident in the way that stepping into the bathtub causes the phone to ring. My photographer friend, Jonathan, a Brit who spoke better Thai than English, worked his way through several bags of crisps. Our driver gave himself a pedicure. We went home at five.

The second night the photographer voiced what I'd been thinking: "Is it okay to want somebody to get hurt or die? I mean, if it's going to happen anyway..."

"Yeah," I said, "and why can't it happen before midnight?"

The call came at midnight. The scene was less than a kilo-meter away, but when we arrived there was only an overturned Vespa and a puddle of blood. The victim had been taken to a hospital by the coppers. A near miss for us, but from the size of the puddle, maybe the last miss for the Vespa driver.

After that, nothing. Same thing the third night. By now I was overdosing on junk food, too, and drinking far too much beer, and the photographer and I were beginning to tell each other the same stories.

The next three nights we shifted gears and hung out in a press room with reporters who cover crime and accidents for the Thai newspapers, who range over the whole city. They watched tele-vision and played cards and the only action was on TV. Jonathan and I wondered if we might hire ourselves out to ward off dan-ger. Obviously, no one got maimed or killed on our watch.

So we returned to the bodysnatchers, who told us about a legendary ten-meter stretch of highway where so many died—it's believed the ghosts of the dead were causing the new accidents. (Where, I wanted to ask, but thought that might seem rude.) Our driver also reminisced about the time when a truck bomb killed nearly a hundred people outside the city; everyone got in on that one, he said.

We were riding with a different Poh Teck Tung unit this time and when we started out at seven o'clock, it was a Friday night and it was raining and it was the last day of the month: payday. For sure, the driver said, we'd get something smeared across the macadam tonight. He predicted at least two serious accidents.

It was nearly midnight when I tried the buy-a-beer trick and with the first mouthful, the driver called, "Let's go!"

Ten minutes of grand prix driving followed, siren announcing our importance, me sitting in the back on the floor with the num-ber two guy, braced as we dodged at high speed through traffic. When we arrived there were two other rescue units on site already (from small, neighborhood foundations), along with a crowd of about two hundred spectators and police, who told us two men were taken away, the driver to a hospital with serious injuries, the other, injured slightly, to the police station to explain why he and his two mates stole the car and then drove it into a concrete telephone pole. A third man was barely conscious and wedged beneath the savagely crushed car's front end and a rescue worker was holding an IV bottle with the drip stuck into the man's arm as others wheeled the "iron jaws" into place to pry open the mangled iron to get to him.

The press was there, too, pushing forward to capture as much blood on film as possible. The police politely moved aside for them. On the way back to the petrol station, the man sharing the floor in the back with me gave me a hearty thumbs up and a happy grin. We settled down to another wait. I bought another beer.

At twelve fifty five a.m., we were off again, this time to where a pickup truck broad-sided a sedan. All drivers and passengers were on the way to a hospital and as we returned to the petrol station there was another call, this one to pick up three corpses, all dead on arrival following the car-truck accident.

The first two bodies, a man and a woman, were laid out on the emergency room floor and were being wrapped in blotting paper to catch the leaking fluids and then were trussed up in a muslin cloth. The third was in another hospital nearby, also on the floor, apparently naked, her body covered with paper toweling, the top of her head a mess, her eyes and mouth open, expressing something between horror and surprise.

Our driver took pictures of the corpses after scrawling their names on a piece of paper and positioning it beneath their chins, like the names held under the arrested in police photographs. In this case, the final I.D. was taken lying down.

One at a time, the bodies were carried to the ambulance where they were fingerprinted and stacked in the rear. I squeezed into the front with the photographer and the number two guy hunkered down with the corpses in the back.

At three a.m., we arrived at the Wang Tong Lung police station, where our guys dragged the bodies to the rear of the vehicle one at a time and opened the top end of the muslin wrappings so a cop could take pictures with his little point-and-shoot camera. I was reminded how the Thais so love to take pictures (no matter what the occasion) and wondered if the cop showed these to his friends over drinks. One of the bodies had to be removed from the rescue unit to get at the others, causing a head wound to re-open and send blood running into the street, providing something of interest for the stray dogs in the morning, perhaps. In an apartment building opposite, a half-dozen people stood on verandahs in their pajamas and watched. This probably was a nightly occurrence for them; better than Thai TV.

Once the pictures were taken, the cop returned to watch a football game on the station house TV and after re-stacking the corpses, our guys spent half an hour filling out forms. Jonathan, who'd been here before on assignment for another magazine, told me it's the same for homicides, the corpses scraped off the floors or lifted from beds or bathtubs, wherever murder or suicide occurs: the cops let Poh Teck Tung do all the paper work.

At four a.m., at last we were at the end of the evening's bloody highway, where the bodies were transferred to stainless steel gurneys and wheeled into the morgue at Police General Hospital. There they became statistics and in the morning, relatives would be notified if any could be found.

It Didn't Happen Because I Wasn't There

Several years ago, when I was researching a story about foreign movie-making in Thailand, I was invited to visit the set of *Cutthroat Island*, a Hollywood-style pirate flick starring Geena Davis and Matthew Modine then being filmed in Krabi. The day before I was to leave Bangkok, my visit was cancelled and I was told that bad weather had caused the shoot to fall behind schedule, prompting the director to close the set to all visitors.

Later, I learned the truth. The film's assistant director had jumped out of a hotel window to his death and the Hollywood film company didn't want the story to leak out. Nor, of course, did the hotel or the Tourism Authority of Thailand.

How could an assistant director of a motion picture produced by a major American film company commit suicide in such a dramatic manner and the story not get into the press, at least locally? Easy. The police were paid to keep a lid on their reports, and if some lucky or enterprising local reporter stumbled onto the story, he was taken to lunch and given a fat envelope, too.

This sort of thing occurs all the time in Thailand. It's a variation of the old story about a tree falling in a forest with no one present to hear it, so did it make a sound? If there's nothing in the press or on TV, it didn't happen. Dozens of foreign visitors die in hotels and restaurants and while shopping every year and rarely is there any news of it. In late summer of 2001, a friend returned from Koh Tao, telling me that the bodies of two foreigners washed ashore not far from where he was staying, one of them missing his feet and hands, but there was nothing in the press about it. In the eight years I've lived in Bangkok, I know of half a dozen foreign deaths, heart attacks and suicide being the most common cause, and they went unreported, too. Why? It might adversely affect tourism in some way. The police notify the relevant embassy and the embassy handles the case like a pussycat buries its poop.

Another, more shocking example of what I'm talking about came a few years ago when there was a serious outbreak of dysentery, causing a number of deaths and more than a hundred hospitalizations. Do you think anyone was warned away from the epidemic area? The press was told that there had been some diarrhea, that's all. While tourism proceeded undisturbed.

A more recent case—perhaps the worst of all—surfaced in 2003 and 2004 when bird flu swept across much of Asia, resulting in the death of hundreds of millions of chickens and many humans as well. As was later learned, the first chickens died in Thailand in October, 2003. It was established as early as November that the disease was indeed bird flu, but Thailand's first report to the World Organization for Animal Health was not submitted until January 23, 2004. By that time, over ten million birds had been slaughtered. Up to that point, the truth was covered up as government spokesmen blamed cholera and bronchitis, common diseases that wipe out chicken flocks fairly frequently.

Why? It was, as reported by Kavi Chongkittavorn, an editor of *The Nation* (Jan. 26, 2004) "feared that the news would cause panic among farmers and damage the national economy. Last year," he continued, "Thailand exported poultry worth US$1.75 billion a year to Japan and the rest of world. After all, the disease's discovery came hot on the heels of the government's confident announcement that economic growth in 2004 would ratchet up to eight percent. Anything deemed damaging to this noble goal had to be swept under the carpet."

It wasn't until the truth was revealed—and numerous countries banned imports of poultry from Thailand—that the government shifted gears. In his opening address to an international conference on the bird flu on Jan. 29, Thailand's prime minister acknowledged that "mistakes and errors" had been made in the handling of the crisis, but insisted that his administration was committed to full transparency in combating the problem.

Thus it might have come as a surprise to some when just six months later, in July, 2004, as the disease returned to Thailand's flocks, the Livestock Development Department again failed to issue a warning. The earlier cover-up had resulted in a huge public relations disaster and one had to wonder why officials took the same tack again. Livestock chief Yukol Limlaemthong had an imaginative response and was quoted in the *Bangkok Post* (July 7, 2004) as saying, "We did not inform the public about the new outbreak because we assumed that Thai people no longer care about the re-emergence of bird flu, which has become an ordinary incident here."

Had enough? Wait. There are two phrases that appear in the press, so often, in fact, they've become amusing cliches. Whenever there is a highway accident involving a bus or truck and there is numerically significant loss of life, as happens more frequently than people living outside Thailand might believe possible, the story in the newspapers almost always includes the sentence, "The driver fled the scene."

I've seen this happen, even without loss of life involved. I was in a taxi stopped in traffic when the truck driver in front of us for some reason reversed his vehicle and backed the rear of the truck onto the hood of the cab. By the time the cabbie had reached the truck cabin, the door was swinging wide and the truck driver was long gone, as if he'd said while fleeing, "I wasn't there, so it didn't happen, erase, erase, erase."

The second sentence appears in crime stories when the charges filed against a prominent person are dropped, as almost in every case they are. Why? "Insufficient evidence."

Some more of the denial is cosmetic. When the World Bank chose Bangkok for a meeting of ten thousand delegates in 1992, the city erected a US$92-million convention center named for the

Queen and then issued eviction orders to residents of an adjacent slum. When residents threatened to stage a noisy protest outside the meeting hall, a compromise allowed them to stay so long as bright murals were painted on the corrugated walls of their shacks. The government also banned all vendors from sidewalks and declared a public holiday to make it appear that the city didn't have a traffic problem. (Thereby clearing the air somewhat, as well.) The same ploy has been used for other international gatherings.

My favorite came in 2003 when Thailand hosted the Asia Pacific Economic Council (APEC) and a special Royal Barge Procession was staged on the Chao Phrya River. Delegates were to view this impressive cultural display from the Thai Navy's headquarters on the west side of the river. On the opposite side was a slum, so the Bangkok Metropolitan Administration, in a last-minute effort to enhance the capital's landscape, erected what arguably was the world's largest banner. It featured an image of the Grand Palace and welcomed the delegates to lovely Bangkok. Over half a kilometer in length and about the height of a four-story building, the slum was thus disappeared.

Thailand is not alone in donning the loose robes of denial when it feels better than the restrictive girdle of fact. Denial is a handy state of mind for people in all walks of life in all corners of the planet for every reason imaginable. Criminals routinely deny everything that seems threatening to their reputations and freedom. Parents deny that they have a drug or alcohol dependency, or a problem at home with the kids. Scapegoats are found for mistakes in business or on the sports playing field. On a larger scale, mass killings, even genocide, go unreported.

"It wasn't me" and "It wasn't my fault" seem to be ingrained in whatever part of the brain or moral code that has anything to do with assuming responsibility. Disavowal or refutation of any charge, no matter how large or small, seems as automatic a response as the kick that comes when a doctor taps a rubber hammer on a person's knee.

Some call denial cowardice, but truly it is only an act of survival, a simple tactic used by the guilty for millennia. Richard

Nixon and Bill Clinton and many more were caught with their pants down, either figuratively or literally, have sought similar refuge. Remember, "I am not a crook"? And, "I did not have a sexual relationship"? In those cases, the truth eventually prevailed.

Thailand, on the other hand, seems to have mastered denial in ways challenged only, perhaps, by the Japanese. (Another story for another time.) For it is here, in the Land of Smiles, where, contrary to all the tee-shirts that say otherwise, shit doesn't happen. Or if it does, it's not brown and it doesn't stink.

A couple of years ago, there was a big controversy over whether or not school history books should be updated to include the pro-democracy demonstrations of May 1992 that led to soldiers shooting protestors in the street, leaving more than a hundred dead or missing. Twelve years later, the whereabouts of the missing were still not known and official reports reluctantly released to the public under a new freedom of information act were heavily censored, with the names of officers in charge of the action blacked out. The *Bangkok Post* described it as "hidden violence in a culture of peace."

After much to-ing and fro-ing, with liberals and academics demanding the truth about what happened and those responsible still trying to cover their asses and save their collective face, Education Minister Panja Kesornthong held a press conference. After a long and sincere contemplation, he announced that the ministry had decided not to include anything about the incidents in the new textbooks then being prepared because, he said, with a straight face, it "wasn't history."

And why wasn't it history?

Because, the minister explained, all the people involved in the tragic events weren't dead yet.

Funny Business

The Rubber Barons

When I was growing up in the United States, the word "rubber," in the plural, referred to overshoes you pulled onto your feet when it rained. In association with the word "check," it meant you had insufficient funds in the bank and the check bounced. Affix it to another word and "rubberneck" meant to look about or stare with curiosity.

Some friends of my parents played a "rubber" of bridge, meaning a round or series of play until one side won two out of three games. In the United Kingdom, it was the word used for eraser, because they were made from rubber and when they fell off your school desk they bounced all over the classroom floor.

As I entered adolescence, the word gained a deeper meaning, it being the most common euphemism in America for a condom, because it too was made from what my dictionary calls "the highly elastic solid substance obtained from the milky juice of various tropical trees and plants." Some of those little packets that American adolescents like me carried in their wallets until they fell apart (unused) said "Made in Thailand." Now I live in Thailand, so I decided to go to the source.

Welcome to Trang, the first place a rubber tree was planted in Thailand almost exactly one hundred years ago, in 1899, (brought from Indonesia by the provincial governor, although the rubber tree originated in Brazil). Today, rubber is the nation's second largest agricultural product after rice, thriving in the

Kingdom's humid climate so well that it is the world's third largest exporter, following Malaysia and Indonesia.

In Trang, as in much of the nation's southern peninsula, there are vast stands of rubber, where trees lined up like sentries form long, dark tunnels and men still go out before dawn with miner's lamps on their heads to make foot-long diagonal cuts in the bark, placing a plastic bowl at the bottom of the "tap" to catch the dripping sap. Two hours later, the bowls are emptied, the white gooey latex is stored in plastic barrels for a day, then poured into what look like deep baking trays and mixed with sulfuric acid to aid coagulation, forming malleable pillows which are then flattened by hand and (literally) foot. Finally, they are pushed through hand-cranked metal rollers and draped over bamboo poles in the yard to dry, looking like bleached doormats. Five days later—assuming it doesn't rain—the now translucent mats are taken in the family pickup truck or on the back of a motorbike to collection points and sold by the kilo.

The work hours are long, starting as early as midnight on some of the larger plantations and continuing through much of the day. The labor is also unpredictable. The latex flows best when the weather is cool and the air is still. Warmer, windier weather is not so good and you can't cut when it rains or the leaves fall, or in the spring when the new leaves are coming in. This means tappers may sometimes work only 120 to 160 days a year.

Nor is it always an attractive investment for landowners, who must wait five to seven years before a tree is ready for tapping, and replant every twenty-five to thirty years. Rubber grows better in poor soil than do cash crops such as sugarcane and maize, but the work is as labor-intensive today as it was when the business was growing up with the new automobile industry. And with world economies bouncing like, well, a rubber ball, market prices are unpredictable, too. In 1999, the slump in economies worldwide plus stiff competition drove the price in Thailand well below break-even.

Kam Nuchitsiripatra is a third-generation rubber planter who knows the market well. His grandfather migrated to Thailand from China in 1917. By the time Kam was fourteen he could "tap" eight hundred trees in a day, so he hired someone to collect the latex as he continued to cut and asked his grandfather for fifty percent of the earnings. At sixteen, he introduced a stronger, more productive strain of tree to Trang and sold cuttings from the new trees to other farmers. Stick one of the cuttings into plain red earth and in six weeks you had a plantable tree.

Kam is called "famous" in Trang province. Besides the thousand or so mature trees his workers tap on land he owns outside the city, he still has a backyard "farm" in town where he sells cuttings. As head of the local rubber planters association, he is also a storehouse of facts. There are six million acres (2.3 million hectares) of rubber in Thailand, spread across twenty-two provinces, mainly in the south, he says, a half-million of the acres in Trang. The export of rubber currently brings about US$2 billion to Thailand annually, and a family makes about US$1,750 a year. Rubber may once have made millionaires of colonial plantation owners (in what was then called Indochine, Indonesia, and Malaya), but today the world price is so low, Thailand's government pays farmers to replant.

Choosit Lee, another third-generation rubber worker, is the factory manager at Sri Trang Agro-Industry, where in a warehouse larger than two airplane hangers about four hundred tons of the latex sheets are washed and dried every day, then graded and bundled for resale, a job he holds, in part, because he speaks Mandarin, Cantonese, and two southern Chinese dialects, Thai, Malay, English, and Japanese; his company sells to factories around the world, making him handy to have around when the phone rings. He is teaching his two young children Mandarin and English, but they, he insists with a laugh, probably won't be interested in following in their father's footsteps when it's time to choose a career.

As on the plantation, he tells me, in the factory, too, little has changed in a hundred years. There are forklifts now, and regular coffee breaks for the employees, but much is still Dickensian, reminiscent of an earlier, harsher era. Here, in a building six acres in size, endless piles of rubber sheets on pallets are brought to the ends of massive cement tubs full of water for washing. Men throw armloads of the sheets into the waist-deep water and other men inside the tubs wearing only shorts hold on to bamboo scaffolding overhead and stomp on the floating mats to separate mold and other external impurities, kicking the mats forward to where women standing in the water flip them one by one between rollers to remove the surface water. The pace is frantic and the noise and water splashing recalls a public wading pool for children on a hot summer day. But you know this isn't fun.

As the sheets come through the rollers, they're draped over bamboo racks, taken by forklift and stacked ten meters high in metal rooms for smoking, to remove the last moisture inside the rubber. Five days later, the sheets emerged baked to a golden brown and smelling eerily like kippers, or smoked herring, the popular English breakfast dish.

Now embedded bits of dirt, insects and air bubbles are cut away by hand with scissors and the sheets are graded individually according to the quality of what's left. The cleanest rubber is graded highest and is sold for the best price to firms making tires for airplanes and luxury automobiles. The coarser stuff is used for truck tires and everything left over, including the bits cut out of the sheets with the dirt, is turned into rubber slippers.

Like the pig, where everything is used except for the squeal, little of the rubber tree is wasted. The wood, lightweight and easy to work with, as well as abundantly available, is made into furniture and toys, from dollhouses to blocks to spinning tops. Because Thailand has banned the logging of most trees, rubber wood now accounts for seventy percent of raw materials for the country's wooden furniture industry.

There's also a market for the liquid latex, brought to the factory in tanker trucks. Choosit Lee takes me to a rise on the property, one of the highest points in the province, he says. Below and stretching to low mountains miles away are the countless rows of trees. Here, a cargo that looks like melted vanilla ice cream is pumped into company trucks and transported to nearby Hat Yai, where hand-sized molds are dipped into it to form rubber gloves, ubiquitous around the world.

In ways too numerous to count, this stuff thus plays a role in more people's lives than possibly any other man-made product, save perhaps steel and electricity. Remove rubber from the earth and you lose what must be history's favorite toy, the ball, you leave most land and air vehicles without tires and inner tubes, and homes and offices and shops go wanting the rubber band, while children are denied something with which to correct mistakes and party balloons to blow up.

Without rubber, we'd have to get along without hot water bottles, life rafts, bathing caps, foam mattresses, raincoats and other all-weather gear, wetsuits for divers and surfers, garden hoses, gaskets and seals and fan belts for cars and buses and trucks, airport conveyor belts, door and car mats, baseballs (the cores are rubber), basketballs, and ping-pong paddles. Bureaucracy everywhere would stumble to a clumsy halt without a rubber stamp. And as for all those you-know-whats essential to family planning and world health, they'd probably be made of plastic or something even unfriendlier.

They are not made in Trang, by the way. Most of those factories are in Chon Buri. Another story for another time.

Thailand's Beer Wars

There must be a hundred ways to rate a country as "world class," but my favorite is in the answer to this question: Does it have a great beer? So I guess it wasn't Thailand's "greatness" that led me to move there. Even before I visited the country, I didn't like its beer. In fact, I thought it was quite horrible.

At the time, in the 1980s, I was living in Honolulu where there was a Thai restaurant that imported what was commonly regarded as Thailand's "national" beer. That was because from the 1930s onwards, the government had given a monopoly to the Boon Rawd Brewery Company Limited of Bangkok, makers of a lager called Singha.

Based on a recipe and technology from Germany and made from locally grown barley and imported hops, the beer whose name meant "lion" (an animal never seen in Asia) had a high alcohol content of six percent and, for my money, too many of those female hop flowers that gave the brew its bitter taste. Of course, it could have been the water, always a determining factor in a beer's flavor. Singha had its brewery alongside the polluted Chao Phyra River and drew its water from artesian wells, sunk deep beneath the swampy ground on which the city was built, creating an image that was less than reassuring.

When I bellied up to my first Thai bar in 1993, Singha controlled ninety percent of the market and two other locally produced beers, Kloster and Amarit, franchises from the German brewer Beck's, competed for what was left, mainly selling to tourists and expatriates. Both had less alcohol than Singha and neither had its acrid bite. When in Bangkok, I drank Kloster. However, when I traveled outside the city, there was no choice. If you didn't drink Singha, you didn't drink beer. And even if you'd brought some other brand with you and wanted to cool it with ice—in Thailand, men customarily put ice in their beer—the frozen water available was of extremely dubious origin.

Then came one of the greatest shifts in the history of beer marketing. In under ten years, not only were dozens of brands made available, Singha, once in privileged command, was left hanging out to dry with only eleven percent of the market, while an upstart newcomer called Chang (Thai for "elephant") had a whopping seventy percent! How that was accomplished is not taught in reputable business schools, nor likely would the tactics survive any court test in the developed world. It was, on the other hand, a classic story that illustrated perfectly how trade was conducted in Thailand: ruthlessly.

It was a war waged by two families, one led by a man of inherited riches who coaxed royalty to captain his board, the other by a man with a fourth grade education, the son of a vendor who sold oysters on the street. If novelist James Clavell were alive, this cast of characters and their books of dirty tricks would have offered him material for a sequel to *Tai-pan* and *Shogun*.

Boon Rawd, the makers of Singha (or "Singh," as its loyal drinkers say), was established in 1934 by Phraya Birombhakdi, whose son Prajuab was sent to study beer culture in Germany's Domen Institute, returning to look after the Singha monopoly. When he died, Santi and Piya Bhirombhakdi took command. For more than half a century, through the Japanese occupation of Thailand and into the 1960s and 1970s when Americans built air bases and ports and roads for the transport of bombs and outdrank the thirstiest of Thais in noisy go-go bars, and thence into the boom years of the 1980s and early 1990s when the Kingdom was listed in the *Guinness Book of Records* as having the world's fastest growing economy, Singha was never challenged. The family had built its business on connections with the aristocracy and for a time Adulkit Kittiyakara, brother of Her Majesty the Queen, served as company chairman. Further competition was not allowed. And sales went up, up, up.

Then along came the oyster vendor's son, Charoen Sirivadhanabhakdi, whose company was given a monopoly of his own, being awarded by the Finance Ministry licenses to all twelve regional whisky distilleries—"whisky" so called but made from fermented rice and sugar cane and thus, in fact, a rum. In rural Thailand, where seventy percent of the population lived, the preferred drink was one of Charoen's products, named for the Mekhong River that flanked part of the country's borders with Laos and Cambodia. This drink was colored brown with caramel for the city folk and left "white" (clear) for the rural market, and it was cheaper than beer by far.

Deciding to take on Singha's dominance, Charoen formed a partnership with Carlsberg when the beer giant from Denmark was given permission to enter Thailand. The original formula was changed, increasing the alcohol content and bitterness, and the international price was reduced—but it still cost more than Singha. They claimed a price premium went with the beer's international status. New brand, higher price: one thing was very clear—if Carlsberg wanted to topple Singha, it had to sell in volume. Thus, began a marketing war unlike any seen in Thailand before.

Charoen ordered his sales network to push Carlsberg along with all his whiskies, including Saengthip as well as Mekhong, and to tell any Singha agent (retailer) declining to take the beer that it couldn't buy the popular whisky. The genteel Bhirombhakdi family then told its more than ten thousand agents nationwide that if they so much as sold a single bottle of Carlsberg, they'd lose the right to sell Singha. It was what was called in another part of the world a "Mexican stand-off." It didn't last long. Upcountry, if you couldn't get the whisky your customers wanted, you were, effectively, out of business and as a result, the Singha distribution system disintegrated.

Some later said this was a diversionary tactic, that Charoen all along had planned to introduce a purely "local" brand. Hadn't he obtained two licenses to produce beer, after all? In any case, in 1994, this is what he did, launching Chang, a brew with a higher alcohol content (6.4 percent compared to Singha's six percent) and a price so low it didn't even cover production costs, creating a product that literally delivered more bang for the baht and demanded the attention of the budget beer drinker.

How could he do this and survive? He nearly doubled the price of the whisky and bundled whisky sales and beer sales together: in order to get the whisky, a retailer had to take the package. If you wanted to buy twenty liters of the whisky most popular in the countryside, you also had to buy four cases (forty-eight big bottles) of Chang. In this fashion, the beer loss was covered by the increased cost of the whisky...and the entire nation was saturated with the strongest, cheapest beer ever marketed.

In time, this led many drinkers to change from Charoen's whisky to his beer. He didn't care. It was like taking money out of one pocket and putting it in the opposite one. The primary result is that Chang came to dominate the beer market as Singha's share fell like a bungee jumper. By the end of 1995, Chang acquired seven percent of the market as Singha retreated to eighty two. Chang's slice of the pie jumped to fourteen percent in 1996, thirty one percent in 1997, thirty two percent the next year, and to more than sixty percent in 1999, sinking Singha's "one nation, one beer" marketing slogan once and for all.

That was the year that Boon Rawd yelled foul to the newly formed Trade Competition Board, a part of the Commerce Ministry. "We lodge the complaint because we want to make the first case under the Competition Law, and we want it to be a case study on unfair trade practices which are widespread in Thailand," said Santi Bhirombaskdi, the man whose family held a virtual monopoly on beer production and sales for more than sixty years and forbade its agents to buy Chang when it was introduced. The irony likely was not lost on Dr. Supachai Panichpakdi, then the former commerce minister (and later the chief of the World Trade Organization). In his ruling, Charoen and Chang won the day.

One anti-trust officer said it was obvious that the distiller had resorted to predatory pricing, an unfair practice where one company, usually a big one with deep pockets, sells its product at an unsustainable low price calculated to cause its competitors, especially smaller ones, to bleed red ink until they went out of business. So what Charoen did might have been unfair, but it wasn't clear, the board ruled, that it was illegal according to existing statute.

Boon Rawd did what it could to pick up the pieces, introducing brands called Leo (named not for the lion, but the spotted leopard, another big cat never seen in Thailand) and Super Leo, and then Super Lion to replace Super Leo, subsequently phasing out Super Lion and reintroducing it as Thai Beer. It also launched Singha Gold (a light beer) and then in 2004, Singha 70 to mark its seventieth anniversary. It hired an ad agency to produce a series of TV commercials exposing Chang's questionable marketing practices and then enlisted three Thai boxing legends to endorse the beer in another series of spots. (A reaction to Chang's using Ad Carabao, Thailand's most popular rock musician.) It sponsored an Emmy nominated Thai cooking show in the United States. It launched a blend of beer with tequila. Finally, it reduced Singha's strong alcohol content and bitter "hoppy" taste.

As beer consumption increased in Thailand, Singha sales by unit count improved, but in 2001, Chang's market share was at seventy five percent, and Singha and Leo each stood at eleven per cent.

That was the year that Chang delivered the unkindest cut and proposed a merger of the companies. It would be a "merger of equals," said the oyster vendor's son, with each firm owning fifty percent. Santi surprised no one when he said it was "impossible both from the heart and for business reasons." Chang was in a stronger financial position and had the better distribution network, so who, Santi surely asked himself, would end up running the show? Besides, he said, the government probably would reject such a proposal as being too monopolistic. Instead, Santi announced he was seeking an alliance with a foreign brewer to help with his large debt load and lost market share and to improve the company's export capability.

As the beer market continued to open up, more new local brands and international labels gained distribution and by 2004 the supermarket where I shopped had six local beers and a surprising twenty-two imports from ten countries (some of them locally produced under franchise): Tiger from Singapore; Victoria Bitter, Fosters, and Crown Lager from Australia (plus a beer-tequila mix called Mez); Budwiser and Miller from the United States; Corona from Mexico; Asahi from Japan; Heineken and Grolsch from the Netherlands; Strongbow and Chimay from Belgium (the latter brewed by Trappist monks); Menabrea from Italy; Guinness from Ireland; and Kloster, Weihenstephaner, Erdinger, Veltins, Furstenberb,Warsteiner, and Diebels from Germany.

By 2004, Charoenhad put his children in charge of the beer business as he diversified, acquiring the local offices of the John Hancock Life Insurance and Southeast Insurance, a service affiliate of Bangkok Bang, Berli Jucker (originally a Swiss company and now Thailand's largest bottle maker), and NCC Management Company, which operated the Queen Sirikit National Convention Centre. He also owned the Hotel Plaza Athenée, the Imperial Queen's Park Hotel and other hotels in the Imperial Group, a controlling stake in the Lao Brewery in Vientianne, and Dho-Spaak Communication, the holder of the World Cup broadcasting rights in Thailand.

Singha was hanging in there. Sales of Singha, Beer Thai, and a mid-priced brew called Mittweida introduced to compete with Heineken hadn't much improved, but the Bahirombhakdi family survived Charoen's assault on its control of the bottled water market and in 2004, one of the more visible heirs, a grandson of the founder, surfaced on an interesting quest. Chutinant Bhirombhakdi was perhaps best known as a keen sportsman, a promoter of the martial art tae kwon do and a handgun sharpshooter. In 2003, he also acted in a television series. The next year he enrolled in class in the National Defense College, an elite military school that gave business executives, civil servants, and social leaders a chance to return to academic life.

Participants had to write a thesis and Chutinant picked as his subject Thailand's competition law. In an early draft, quoted in *The Nation* (Apr. 7, 2004), he wrote that "...Thailand has been on its way to amending, adapting and adopting international trade practices since the days of King Rama V...The Trade Competition Act of 1999 is the latest revision concerning domestic markets, which are now under international scrutiny. But since its inception, many feel that the Act has not had as big an impact as originally envisioned, lacking major substance."

I'm sure he's right. Surely he has a reason to think that.

As for me, I drink Chang. I can find it just about everywhere, it suits my tastes better than Singha, it still has the kick of a mule, and it's cheaper than all the rest.

But, sorry to say, it ain't a world-class beer.

Faking It

In the final months of 2001, a lot of Thais raised hell about an American scientist who was alleged to have sneaked some of Thailand's delicious jasmine, or *hom mali*, rice back to the United States, where he planned to mess with its genes and patent it. Why you should get a patent on something Mother Nature provides, with or without genetic modification, I don't fully comprehend, but the issue here is that many Thais were furious...as they were again in 2004 when it was learned that genetic tests on rice cultivated in and marketed by neighboring Cambodia was identical to that grown across the border in its Thai birthplace.

The fear of "stolen" rice is not the only fret. The government's Intellectual Property Department's knickers also were in a twist over complaints about the liberal use of the words *phad Thai* overseas to describe the traditional local noodle dish. No sooner was that out of the headlines—it was concluded that protection of fried noodles was a lost cause—than concerned citizens started worrying about guarding the name and model of the *samlor*, or *tuk-tuk*, the noisy little three-wheeled vehicles that dart in and out of traffic mainly in areas popular with tourists and shoppers.

Again, it seemed to be too late, as *tuk-tuk* trademarks had been taken out in several foreign countries. A British company that imported the vehicles, MMW Imports, already was modifying and selling them under the MMW Tuk Tuk brand. The company, which declined to reveal the identity of its Thai supplier, was upgrading the *tuk-tuks* to the standards required to run on European highways—no easy task, according to the firm's boss— thereby creating, in effect, a new vehicle.

What made these stories about Thailand and charges of alleged theft interesting was the Thais' hostile response to the idea that someone might be stealing from them. While at the same time, Thailand was one of the centers of international theft, a country where virtually everything was counterfeited and sold on the open marketplace.

Walk down Sukhumvit Road, where I live, and you can buy clothing by Polo and Camel, Swiss army knives, Nike and Reebok sports shoes, and tee-shirts advertising the Hard Rock Cafe and popular English football clubs. There are at least fifty stores where Indian proprietors (who also own much of the real estate) sell knock-off designer suits, measured on the spot and slapped together with a second fitting a few hours later, delivery in less than a day—stitched by hundreds of poor citizens and immi-grants (both legal and otherwise) sitting at rows of sewing machines in factories the length of football fields on the city's industrial fringe. There's even a store on Sukhumvit called Versaces; I suppose the owner thinks the "s" at the end of the name circumnavigates any smear of illegitimacy. Markets and street stalls and shops in fancy malls from Chiang Mai to Pattaya to Phuket offer more—Rolex watches, French perfumes, the newest movies, DVDs, video games, gold jewelry, Gucci purses, even, god help us, Viagra. Every item a fake.

"The Thais are not innovators," a friend says. "They created one of the best cuisines in the world, taking a little of this and that from here and there—the chilis from Portuguese traders, the curries from India—and made it something unique. Beyond that, there isn't much to brag about. That may sound unkind, but the truth is, what Thailand is good at is copying. With or without permission."

To some, this means counterfeiting. Violating international intellectual property laws. Stealing. The simplest word is theft and the most popular word in the press is "piracy."

An effort was exerted to halt this. Police arrested thousands of vendors a year and in 2003 shut down nineteen factory owners; photographs appeared regularly in the press showing phoney products being flattened by heavy equipment. (Leading many counterfeiters operating in malls to employ spotters at the mall entrances who send an alert by cell phone when the cops show up, causing thousands of counterfeit discs to disappear from open view.) When the United States threatened to delay Free Trade Area negotiations with Thailand if the Thai government failed to make progress on intellectual property issues, the prime minister said he had thirteen state agencies involved in the suppression of copyright violations. Thailand further offered US$25,000 to informants for compact disc copying machines and cops were promised more than five U.S. cents for every pirated CD seized. Even when a coalition of popular performers appealed to their fans to stop buying bogus CDs, because the forgers were making it impossible for them to earn a living, the effort was ineffectual.

The counterfeit trade remained so untouched, in fact, that local producers cut prices, between twenty and fifty percent for CDs and VCDs and the license holder for such cartoon characters as Snoopy, Popeye and Garfield re-priced their product to five percent above the fakes—giving consumers some insight as to how large the original profit margins had been and why so much bootlegging was going on in the first place. It was, both pirates and consumers agreed, as if a Southeast Asian sort of Robin Hood were stealing from the rich to give the poor.

This cuts to the core of the matter. When a copy of Microsoft Office for an individual user cost over 15,000 baht, and Windows, the basic operating system, was sold at almost 10,000 baht, and a copy of the photo-editing software Adobe Photoshop went for 30,000 baht, and the average Thai university graduate entering the civil service received a starting monthly salary of 6,400 baht, it should have no great surprise to anyone when the copied software found a ready market.

Nowhere was this clearer than in one of the least known and most intriguing museums in Bangkok, in the offices of Tilleke &

Gibbons International Ltd., which, despite its *farang* name, is the oldest law firm in Thailand, owned and operated by Thais. The firm has what it calls an "intellectual property" team and here is displayed in some of the hallways the evidence from hundreds of cases, some 1,500 exhibits in all. The thing that struck me the first time I saw it was how diverse the items were. The purses and belts, the cosmetics, the clothing, the watches, the music, the stuff you see on the street I expected. But pharmaceuticals? (Oh, yes, I was assured; did I realize how much ersatz Viagra was sold each day in Bangkok?) Electric irons? Johnny Walker Black? Cigarettes? Laundry detergent? Automobile tires? Engine parts? Motor oil? Veterinary medicine?

Thailand is not alone, of course. Throughout Asia and in other parts of the "developing" world, counterfeit goods are as much a part of the marketplace as exotic fruits and vegetables and live catfish flopping in plastic tubs. According to annual studies by the industry trade group, Business Software Alliance, Vietnam and China lead the world with the highest level of pirated software—including CDs, videos, and games—at an astonishing ninety nine percent. That meant that for every legitimate disc or video for sale in those countries, ninety-nine fakes were on the market, and being sold at a fraction of the legal market price.

So good were the Vietnamese at counterfeiting, that in 2000, the Ministry of Culture and Information announced that local painters duplicated international masterpieces so believably, that from that time forward they had to make the copies three centimeters smaller or larger than the originals. And sign their work under the copied signatures of the original masters. At the time, a credible "Van Gogh" was going for about US$250.

Similarly in China, the porcelain market was doing so well, skilled potters were producing fake Ming, Qing and Song pieces that were fooling some of the experts.

Thailand was not far behind. There were in Bangkok and Ayutthaya sculptors so skilled they produced convincing copies of religious statuary, while others carved wooden figures and, after burying them in the ground and treating them with various chemicals, sold them as the real thing. Years before moving here, I once visited Thailand with a developer from Hawaii who wanted to purchase authentic artifacts for display in his fancy new hotels. Wary of being cheated, he hired a local antiquities scholar, who evaluated the items offered for sale. It wasn't until he returned home that the developer learned his expert okayed bogus items in exchange for a kickback from the counterfeiters.

Most of the piracy is of cheaper items that are mass produced. My son is a computer graphics designer in the U.S. and when he first visited me in Bangkok, I took him to Pantip Plaza, the five-story mall on Petchburi Road devoted mainly to computers and other electronic devices, and software. Our first visit, he was stunned. For an hour or more, all I heard was, "Dad, I paid thirty dollars for that! I paid a hundred dollars for that!" And so on. Never pointing at anything that cost more than a few dollars. When Windows XP, the latest endeavor by Microsoft to separate consumers from their money, appeared in shops the end of 2001, costing almost as much as a PC, copies were flying off the Pantip shelves at two hundred baht (five dollars) apiece.

Even pornography is bootlegged in Thailand. One of the street stalls outside my bank on Silom Road openly sold XXX videos. (The bank moved, the stall remained.) This was just one of several operating in that neighborhood during the day, one of dozens offering the same product at night. The reproduction was sometimes poor—there were incomplete scenes (talk about *coitus interruptus*!), bad focus or color, etc.—but the $2.50 price was right, for a video that cost ten or more times that amount in the country of origin.

Counterfeiting, bootlegging, copying, call it whatever you want, it's practically unavoidable, and so affordable it's irresistible. I'm wearing fake Calvin Klein undershorts. Some of the Polo shirts in my wardrobe are fake. My last pair of slippers said Nike but it was a lie. (And they lasted only two months before falling apart, one of the risks of buying funny goods; there is a joke about the Rolex watch you buy in Bangkok is guaranteed to last as long as it takes to get to the airport on your way home.)

Don't even ask me about my CDs. I'm guilty, guilty, guilty, along with what may be a majority of the urban population.

It's a part of living in Thailand. In the slums, nearly everyone wears designer clothing and you know where it came from. (Ironically, Nike donates a lot of the Real Thing to the Bangkok poor.) The rich keep the legitimate stores going—to be caught wearing a Gucci shirt with imperfect button alignment would be to lose face, after all—but it is that Thai upper class, along with some of the wealthier tourists, who provide a majority of the customers. We poorer folks go for the ersatz goods every time, even if one leg in a pair of "Wrangler" jeans is shorter than the other.

So ingrained is the consumption of fraudulent goods in Thailand that the *Bangkok Post* published a story by two of its reporters (in June 2001) that told readers what to look for in determining not a real thing from a fake, but how to spot the most *convincing* counterfeits.

"Selecting the best fake requires a keen eye," the reporters said.

Bi-Racial Cool

It wasn't so long ago when inter-racial sex was scorned in Southeast Asia and children from such pairings were ostracized. No more. Today, offspring with genes from both east and west are frequently lionized, sometimes winning a spot at the top of their chosen fields, becoming role models as well as celebrities. It is no surprise that this is being exploited commercially, but what isn't admitted so freely is: why?

Until fairly recently, Southeast Asia had an unpleasant history of racial bias. Singapore, Malaysia, Indonesia, Vietnam, Cambodia, Thailand...every nation in the region experienced horrific conflict between various ethnic groups. In some areas, prejudice persists today.

Illegitimate children left behind following war were spurned almost everywhere, notably in Vietnam, Thailand, Laos and the Philippines—wherever the U.S. sent its military. As colonies became nations, mixed-race children were reminders of a Western-dominated past. The most that many could expect was a mean life on the street. So grim was the situation in Vietnam, any mixed-blood youngster who could in any way establish American parentage was given a pass to the United States in order to escape the prejudice; sometimes little more than a western nose or black skin seemed enough to qualify for America's Orderly Departure Program. In Thailand, children of racially mixed parents could not become citizens until the early 1990s.

This prejudice was not exclusively Asian; even in the United States, the last of the miscegenation laws were not overturned until 1965.

Nowadays, the picture has changed, most remarkably in Thailand, where it is no surprise to see headlines in Bangkok's English language dailies that read, "Mixed-race superstars most popular artists" and "Best of Both Worlds." The best example may be Amita Tata Young, the recording and movie star daughter of a Thai woman and her American husband, who serves as Tata's manager. She's been a star since she was eleven, when she won a Thailand Junior Singing Contest. A recording contract and film career followed and in 1998, at age seventeen, she was named by *Asiaweek* as one of Asia's twenty-five most influential personalities and two years later became the first Thai singer to sign a contract with a major American recording company, Sony Columbia. She's also had her face on the world's biggest billboard as Panasonic's Thai spokesperson and in 2004 was linked romantically (but briefly) with an internationally ranked tennis superstar, Paradorn Srichaphan; was castigated by the Thai government's uptight Culture Ministry for a single called "Sexy Naughty Bitchy;" then saw her new CD go platinum within six hours of hitting the stores.

Another, far bigger name whose heritage is split between Thailand and America is Tiger Woods, although to be fair to the son of a Thai woman and a black American ex-soldier, he is a fair golfer whose mixed parentage merely gave his story an added commercial spin. It might be mentioned that Tiger is no favorite in Thailand, thanks to his refusal to leave his five-star hotel to receive an honorary degree from a local university—he had it brought to him!—and lack of interest in anything Thai: not the food, nor the sights, nor the people. This, despite the fact that he was paid a million U.S. dollars to come to Thailand and all he had to do in return was play eighteen holes of a game he was alleged to enjoy.

There are many more who are lesser known outside the region. Nicole Theriault and Peter Corp Dyrendal, topped "The Global Sex Survey 1999—A Youth Perspective" in Thailand, conducted by London's condom manufacturer, Durex. Nicole has an American father, too, and Peter's dad is from Denmark. Another new star, appearing in two films in Thailand, is Ananda Everingham, using the professional name Ananda Eve; mom is from Laos, dad is from Australia, and Ananda grew up in Bangkok, where his father runs a successful magazine publishing company.

There are so many, in fact—in modeling as well as in television, music, and film—that a phrase, *luuk khrung* (literally meaning "half-children"), was added to the language to describe them. When *Time* magazine put what it called the "Eurasian Invasion" (and Tata Young) on its cover Apr. 23, 2001, it said the once-despised offspring controlled an estimated sixty percent of Thailand's entertainment industry, and informed readers that the country once had sent a blue-eyed woman to the Miss World competition, when Sirinya Winsiri, also known a Cynthia Carmen Burbridge, beat out another half-Thai, half-American for the coveted Miss Thailand title.

Of course there's nothing new about this. The "Eurasian" look has been a niche entertainment staple for decades, coming into and going out of fashion several times, not just in Asia but worldwide. France Nuyen, born France Nguyen Vannga of French and Vietnamese-Chinese parents in Marseille, France, starred in Broadway's *The World of Suzie Wong* (1958), for instance, and when Hollywood made the movie two years later, it was another Eurasian, Nancy Kwan, trained as a dancer in the British Royal Ballet, who got the part.

Yet, they were the exception rather than the rule and it wasn't until fairly recently that Asians and part-Asians were considered first for Asian roles; remember the Swedish born Warner Oland as the inscrutable Chinese detective Charlie Chan (in the 1930s), Marlon Brando as an obsequious Japanese servant in *Sayanara* (1957), and Yul Brynner as the strutting King of Siam in *The King and I* (1956)?

It's not been explained satisfactorily why the Eurasian "look" works. When asked, many spout clichés about the meeting of

East and West or, may the gods help us, "globalization." *Time* magazine said Channel V, the Asia-wide music television channel, was one of the first to broadcast the message of "homogenized hybridism," quoting one of the channel's marketing managers as saying, "We needed a messenger that would fit from Tokyo to the Middle East."

The word "exotic" gets mentioned a lot as well, although the meaning of that word is seldom if ever made clear (even in dictionaries). It's further explained that when Asians have some western features, they are more readily accepted by westerners, who are known, historically, for assigning second class status to people with darker skin. As for the Asians, it's easy to say that it's just a part of a global shift toward western style as demonstrated by their avid acceptance of rock music, Hollywood movies, blue jeans, European clothes and cars, Scotch whisky and French wines, KFC and Haagen Dazs. Thailand is famous for embracing western influence and material goods, during its boom years becoming the largest market outside Germany for the Mercedes-Benz, and consuming more Johnny Walker black label than any country other than the United States.

Ananda Eve's father, John, who's lived in Southeast Asia for more than thirty-five years, gets more specific. And he says it's about racial stereotypes.

"It starts with biology," he explains. "In Thailand, and elsewhere, the flat nose and dark skin are considered low class and the straighter nose and lighter skin are more acceptable because they're associated with a higher class. My son was 'discovered' when he was working in a restaurant entirely because of the way he looks. He has his mom's eyes and coloring. He has my nose. He also has a serenity from his mom's Lao side, but it was the look that made him a movie star."

How influential is this new look? Very. For many young people of both sexes all over Asia today western clothing, makeup and other adornment are not enough, so they dye and streak their hair blonde and red, while many young women have their eyes and noses surgically "westernized," and their breasts enhanced. Thailand has some of the best beaches in Asia, but you won't find many Thais there because they don't want a dark skin; many carry umbrellas on sunny days and whitening creams are among the most popular cosmetic products sold, even when health authorities issue grave warnings about how damaging some of them may be for the skin.

Because many of the new stars—in Thailand and elsewhere—have lived and been educated in the West, or attended international schools in Asia, they've been westernized in other ways, too. Thus, some have strong foreign accents and sloppy articulation when they speak or sing in what is supposed to be their native language.

"These people are not Asian any more," says John Everingham.

Thailand–Superlative!

I was heartened when I heard that the powers that be in Bangkok decided to erect billboards boasting that the city has the Longest Place Name in the world, as recognized by the *Guinness Book of Records*. Soon, visitors and residents were to be informed that the city's formal name is (take a deep breath) Krungthepmahanakhon Amonrattanakosin Mahinthar-ayutthaya Mahadilokphop Nopphosin Ratchathaniburirom Udom-rathani-wetmahasa Amonphiman Awatansathit Sakkathatiya Witsanukamprasit.

That's a total of 162 letters and according to the Royal Institute, it means, "City of Angels, Great City of Immortals, Magnificent City of the Nine Gems, Seat of the King, City of Royal Palaces, Home of the Gods Incarnate, Erected by Visvakarman at Indra's Behest." A total of 146 letters, in English, but the Thai words are what count. On maps, this blessedly has been short-ened to Krungthep (City of Angels). The modern name Bangkok means City of Wild Plums.

I'm not sure why this is to be announced on billboards. Do the officials behind the campaign think this will make residents take pride in their capital, or add to the city's exotic reputation and thus increase tourism interest? Or is it—as I hope—a demonstration of some newfound sense of official humor?

Thailand has many superlatives, make no mistake about it. In the Largest Restaurant category, Mang Gorn Luang (The Royal Dragon), a congregation of eating areas spread over four acres of land, with a capacity of five thousand diners who are served by more than one hundred cooks and five hundred servers in national costumes, is the current record holder. So vast is the area, some of the servers wheel about on roller skates, delivering up to three thousand dishes every hour. Surely this is another sign of Thailand's sense of fun, or *sanuk*.

So, too, the world's Largest and Tallest Hotels are in Thailand, the former being the Ambassador City Jomtien, with more than five thousand rooms, the latter being the Baiyoke Sky Hotel, with an observation deck and restaurants on the 77th to 79th floors. From which guests are told they can see the Gulf of Thailand on a clear day. (Another little Thai joke.)

Bangkok also claims the Largest Open Air Market Place, the Chatuchak Weekend Market, an overwhelming shopper's paradise comprising approximately eight thousand stalls spread over thirty acres, where the best advice is if you see something you like, buy it immediately, as you'll never find your way back. And be sure you do your shopping in the morning, before it becomes the World's Hottest and Most Crowded Shopping Complex. This is not a joke.

More serious is the unchallenged record of having the Longest Reigning Royalty. His Majesty Bhumibol Adulyadej (Rama IX), succeeded his older brother on June 9, 1946, putting him at the sixty year mark in 2004 and ahead of the runner-up, England's Queen Elizabeth, who has reigned since 1952.

Bangkok is also home of the Biggest Golden Teak-Wood Building, the 81-room Vimanmet Palace, built in 1901 by King Chulalongkorn (Rama V) as a royal residence. Construction began on an island in the Gulf of Siam, but before completion was moved to Bangkok's Dusit Park near the palace of the present king. There, it served as home for the monarch, his ninety-two wives, and seventy-seven children. Today it's a museum.

And let's not forget the Biggest Gold Buddha Image, located

in an otherwise unremarkable temple, Wat Traimitr, just east of the intersection of Yaowaraj and Charoen Krung Roads in Bangkok, near the city's main railway station. The ten-foot-high statue for many years was covered with stucco and considered unimportant. In 1957, when it was moved to its present location, a transporting sling snapped and the image fell, cracking the stucco covering. Underneath was a solid gold figure, weighing five-and-a-half tons. Historians think it dates from Thailand's Ayutthaya period (1378-1767), when monks likely disguised the image to protect it from Burmese invaders.

All this is well and good and I think such tales would make good billboard copy. However, I also hope that a sense of humor will prevail and Thailand's lesser-known superlatives also get the attention they deserve.

Did you know, for instance, that the Kingdom boasts the Largest Freshwater Fish, the *pla buk* or *pa beuk*, a kind of catfish found in the Mekong River and its tributaries—the biggest documented catch measuring 9 feet, 10.25 inches long and weighing 533.3 pounds? Or the Tallest Stalagmite, rising two hundred feet from the floor of a cave called Tyham Nam Klong Ngu in Kanchanaburi? And let's not overlook the Largest Grasshopper, a species ten inches long and found along the border between Thailand and Malaysia, a boundary it may be seen crossing in fifteen-foot leaps. A couple of them, deep-fried, and you've got yourself a meal. Also not a joke, not in Thailand.

Parents who are unimpressed by their children's hair styles might find comfort in knowing that two brothers in a Hmong village north of Chiang Mai, Yee Sae Tow, age ninety, and Hoo Sae Tow, eighty-eight, have the Longest Hair, measuring 4.84 meters and 5.2 meters, respectively. It's worn deadlock style and carried about like a length of coiled rope.

Probably we shouldn't even talk about Thailand's having the Fastest Economic Expansion and Decline, rising to 9.8 percent in 1995, making it the world's fastest growing economy, then falling to -0.4 percent three years later. And do we really want to talk about the traffic, the humidity and the air?

Decidedly not. That's *not* funny.

Tourism

Bob Levy—not his real name, I'll spare him that—sent me an e-mail to remind me that we'd been university classmates in the United States. He said he and his wife were coming to Thailand and would like to meet me for a drink and whatever. They would be staying at the Oriental Hotel, he said, and because I didn't remember him—it'd been more than forty years since gradua-tion, after all—I asked them to meet me at another nice hotel closer to where I lived, for cocktails in the lobby bar, dinner to follow in an nearby cozy Thai restaurant that specialized in northeastern dishes.

Once our first round of drinks arrived, Bob confessed that he and I never knew each other; rather, he'd seen a story about me in the alumni magazine and figured it might be interesting to spend an evening with me on their first visit to Bangkok. He didn't exactly put it that way, but it was obvious. He was pay-ing for the drinks, so I ordered another and while I didn't like being deceived or patronized, I figured what the hell, it was just one night and maybe he or his wife would be fun to get to know.

You've already guessed. I was wrong.

I won't bore you with the details, just take my word for it when I say it was one of the least interesting and at times most infuriating evenings of my life in Bangkok, many of which are spent entertaining out-of-towners. Over a period of five hours we uncovered nothing we had in common other than the university, about which I had only distant memories.

Worse, they refused to leave the bubble in which they arrived and, from my point of view, they expected to leave the Land of Smiles without much of anything to smile about. Ordering a meal for them—their first taken outside their hotel, they said—was hampered by their belief that Thai food would either (1) poison them, or (2) merely invoke less than amusing damage to their gastro-intestinal systems. The appearance of sticky rice, part of the restaurant's cuisine, actually made them ask if it were possible to get a potato.

The Levys seemed terrified by their excursion. The air was polluted; the traffic was worse than it was back home in Kansas City; the heat and humidity were insufferable; the food looked as if it were alive or, worse, dead; the language was abrasive and undecipherable; the river that ran past their hotel was brown; and they were sure they would contract AIDS from some passing doorknob or toilet seat. Why, I wondered, had they come to Thailand?

As we walked along the *soi* (street) to the main road to catch a cab after dinner, I spotted a small elephant being led by its trainer, who was selling bananas to passers-by, on the opposite side of the street. I thought this offered a perfect opportunity to introduce the Levys to something really Thai, and explained how the animal's native habitat had been destroyed, forcing the elephants to come to the city to beg. They wouldn't go near the tiny beast, practically withdrew *into* the wall in fear (on the opposite side of the street, mind you), and showed visible relief when they clambered into a taxi, to be hurried back to the security of their five-star hotel.

The Levys were what another writer, Carol Hollinger, author of a truly fabulous little book called *Mai Pen Rai Means Never Mind* (1965), called "the 'Humph' people," the visitors to Thailand who greeted each new experience with a "Humph!" of disdain or disgust, the visitors who "stayed at the fancy hotels and hurried down to Jim Thompson's to buy Thai silk." And then went home.

Good riddance, say I, but the Thai government loves these awful people because they spend more money here than other visitors do. The backpackers are welcomed, reluctantly. The sex tourists, too, but never openly. And it's those two visitor categories that give the country much of the reputation that the nation's leaders claim they would like to shed.

In an effort to move in that direction, the Thai government in early 2002 announced plans to create two new tourist destinations that would appeal to the well-heeled traveler. Both schemes were hare-brained, but in Thailand you expected that. One was to turn a relatively unspoiled island in the southeast, Koh Chang, into "another Phuket" (the government's phrase, not mine), but this time for the rich. The intent was to attract the kind of money that Phuket does, without the bars and trashy souvenir shops.

"We want to build a five-star image for Koh Chang by focusing on the environment," said Pornchai Kaemapuckpong, a member of the government's Koh Chang Development Committee. "People coming here should be proud that they can afford its high-end lifestyle." How high-end? The goal was to attract tourists who could spend between US$1,250-1,500 a day. That Koh Chang was a national forest seventy five percent owned by the Royal Forestry Department and that the entire fifty-two-island Koh Chang archipelago was established as a Marine National Park in 1982 appeared to be regarded as irrelevant.

"For many, this has a depressingly familiar ring," Vipasai Niyamabha wrote in The Nation (Feb. 2, 2002). "And just who stands to benefit? We have witnessed parts of Pattaya become another Patpong; Koh Tao like Khao San Road, and Koh Phi Phi another Patong Beach. Is Koh Chang destined to fill her coffers yet lose her soul?"

The other scheme was even crazier. It involved the governments of Thailand, Laos and Cambodia cooperating to construct a five-star resort that would be in what was to be called "The Emerald Triangle," because at the time it was nothing but green jungle located where the three nations meet. The idea was to build a golf course that would allow players to swing their clubs in all three in a single round of play. There were problems, however, one being that much of the territory under discussion was heavily mined from the 1980s, when the Khmer Rouge were fighting in the area.

Major General Kitti Sufksomsatarn, director of the Thailand Mine Action Centre, estimated the cost of the de-mining would be in the neighborhood of US$10.2 million, not including construction of an access road required to reach the site, and take at least a year; he also said that his organization could not assist because the scheme was planned for commercial rather than humanitarian reasons. Talk about the Emerald Triangle stopped.

Why such crazy ideas get any attention at all led inevitably to the doors of the Tourism Authority of Thailand, then a highly politicized arm of the government. In adopting a tourism master plan the same month that these two schemes were announced, the TAT, as it's known, identified five tourism categories, all aimed at the "quality" tourist. These ranged from beaches and islands with potential for development to nature reserves and forests to historical destinations. It was suggested, for instance, that the ancient capital of Ayutthaya be turned into a "living museum" like America's Williamsburg.

That was in 2002, when Thailand called tourism the key sector leading to economic recovery following the Asian meltdown of 1997. In the next two years, the government had to deal with a slew of new challenges both at home and abroad. TAT figures showed arrivals climbed from under seven million in 1995 to almost eleven million in 2002, but that figure fell by more than a million in 2003, thanks to wars in the Middle East, SARS and terrorist incidents in the region. Sunny predictions regarding a comeback in 2004 subsequently were torpedoed by repeated bird flu outbreaks and separatist violence in Thailand's Muslim south.

There were other problems, and these could be longer lasting. In a report to the government, the TAT (quoting *The Nation* on Feb. 25, 2002) concluded that Thailand was "caught in a trap of low prices and profits growth. Although the country welcomes around ten million tourists a year, foreign visitors are spending less time here, and less money, and perhaps looking to alternative destinations such as Vietnam and Cambodia."

Thus, the country was "caught in a vicious circle of being a cheap destination."

Over the years, Thailand's image took other hits so serious they made "cheap" sound almost flattering. Most (in)famously, *Newsweek* (Jul. 12, 1999) said the country's economic advantages over its neighbors were limited to "sex and golf." In 2002, in a special section devoted to Thailand's economy, The *Economist* said two growth industries that merited special attention were "sex and drugs." And in 2004, when the TAT hired a group of researchers at California State University to explore ways the nation might attract more long-stay American tourists, it was told that something had to be done to overcome the perception that the entire country was "dirty, polluted and traffic congested."

Still tourism boomed. Some of the growth could be attributed to the violence and political unrest in other Asian destinations (Indonesia, the Philippines, Nepal, Sri Lanka, Cambodia) or political incorrectness (Myanmar). When terrorist bombs destroyed Bali's tourism in 2002, travelers came to Thailand's southern islands instead. In 2004, a *Lonely Planet* survey named Thailand the number one destination in the world (ahead of Italy, Australia, India, and New Zealand); *Condé Nast Traveler* magazine ranked the Land of Smiles number two (behind Australia) for long-stay visitors and seven out of the top twenty hotels named were in Bangkok, Krabi, Chiang Mai and Phuket.

But there was a basic flaw in the figures. Ten million arrivals per year made Thailand one of the top twenty travel destinations in the world. But more than one of every ten were weekend shoppers and sex tourists from Malaysia who came for what they couldn't get at home. Other repeat "visitors" were long-term foreign residents who left and re-entered to satisfy visa requirements. (I once took a five-hour bus ride to Cambodia eleven times in a single year for that reason, thus was counted eleven times.) Can the tens of thousands of resident business people and their families making frequent exits and re-entries honestly be called "tourists?"

(For the record, according to the Police Department's Immigration Bureau, in 2003, of the ten or so million arrivals counted, 1.3 million came from Malaysia, one million more from Japan, 694,000 from Korea, 650,000 from Hong Kong, 629,000 from Singapore, 624,000 from China, 545,000 from the UK, 521,000 from Taiwan, 459,000 from the U.S., and 379,000 from Germany.)

In addition, there was concern about where the money went, once it was spent. Lisa Mastny, a researcher for Worldwatch Institute in Washington, DC, wrote in *State of the World 2002* that "an estimated ninety percent of the world's tourism enterprises are small businesses, from family-owned restaurants to one-person snorkeling operations. Yet governments are under increasing pressure to grant large-scale investors, including international airlines, hotel chains, and tour operators, easier access to tourism assets. Under a special economic relations treaty with the United States, for example, Thailand must grant companies owned and operated by U.S. investors the same legal treatment as those owned by Thai nationals."

The result? Small, local businesses get crowded out and much of the revenue eventually generated by the big new development goes rushing back out of the country like the withdrawing waves on a beach.

No matter. Travel gurus nowadays advise against sustaining a low-end reputation, and Thailand seems to be going along. Not everyone agrees. Don Ross, a travel writer for the *Bangkok Post*, said in March, 2002, that "moving Thailand out of the cheap tour league might be counterproductive. Rather than raising the country's profile, it might be interpreted as a reason to travel elsewhere." Thailand needs to "keep its eyes on all market segments without belittling one at the expense of another."

On the other hand, should the government manage to change its image and pull in more of the high rollers, the "Humph" people (including the Levys) might come back in force. I have an elephant on the street, standing by.

Country Music, Thai Style

Thirty or forty years ago, a fiery green papaya salad known as *som tam* was called "peasant food." Because it originated in Thailand's impoverished and densely populated, rural northeast, called Isan, it wasn't regarded as fit for "proper" Thai mouths. With the migration of at least a million people from that region—to work in the factories and the tourism and construction industries that fueled much of the country's economic boom—they brought the dish to Bangkok and began selling it from street stalls where others from Isan congregated, near the big hotels, building sites, and in poor residential neighborhoods. In just a few years, it started appearing on mom-and-pop menus and then on "proper" ones, and now it can be found in Thai restaurants around the world and may fairly be called a national dish.

Some people say the same thing could happen to Isan's music. At least, it's now sweeping Thailand, expanding from the niche market it once claimed and going "mainstream," the way the papaya salad did, and the way country music did in the United States.

The comparison to what once was called "hillbilly" music in America is not inappropriate, because the various strains of music from Isan frequently describe the lives and social problems of Thailand's poor the way country music sometimes still does in America, and they are performed emotionally, providing a refreshingly vibrant alternative to the formulaic and instantly forgettable Canto-Pop that fixes so much of the music across Asia, including Thailand. The music itself is characterized by the playing of traditional folk instruments and an insistent keyboard that almost sounds as if there might be a stoned snake-charmer nearby with a basket of sleepy snakes.

Generally, this Southeast Asian country music is called *luuk thung* (pronounced "look tung" and translated "child of the fields"), although there are several variations. Isan borders Cambodia and Laos and the traditions and instruments of the smaller countries have influenced their bigger, more modern neighbor. There are significant differences between Laotian *mor lam* and *mor lam sing* and Khmer *kantruem*, for example, but all generally are put under the *luuk thung* umbrella in the way blue-grass and western swing and other distinct sounds share space on a single *Billboard* country music chart.

Luuk thung first emerged from Thailand's poor central plains and northeast in the 1960s and 1970s about the same time that the United States built air bases in Thailand (several of them in Isan) and Bangkok became a preferred R&R destination for GIs during America's Indochina war. The cultural and political impact of a suddenly intensive foreign presence in Thailand made an impression on the local musicians, as they adopted jeans and tee-shirts, let their hair grow and embraced rock and roll.

The local musicians kept the sound of native instruments of wood and bamboo, however, and lyrics rarely strayed from the problems and causes of the Thais, even when some English phrases were added, as in Carabao's hit, "Made in Thailand," an eco-nationalistic song that told Thais to stop buying stuff made by foreigners. Others took up the cause of the farm girl pressed by poverty into prostitution.

As was true in American country music, the tone often ranged from poignant to angry—success coming from musical talent, but also lyrics that were relatable. Several bands, notably Caravan, strongly identified with Thailand's growing democracy movement, along with leftist balladeers associated with the student uprising of 1972, calling their genre *plaen phua chiwit*, or "Songs for Life."

Luuk thung went into semi-retirement in the 1980s as Thailand experienced a period of military coups, social uncertainty, and massive industrial development, beginning its comeback in the 1990s following a decade of dominance by western recording acts. (Even Michael Jackson appeared in concert in Bangkok during this period.) The revival was fueled in part by the success of Luuk Thung FM, which began broadcasting twenty-four hours a day in 1997. Two years later, the life of Phumphuang Duangchan, known as the Queen of Thai Country Song (think Loretta Lynn or Tammy Wynette), who died in 1992 at age thirty-one, was made into a television mini-series.

A number of odd events occurred during the production of the series, the singer's songs emerging from a computer that wasn't turned on, a missing script that reappeared only after the writer paid her respects to a statue of Phumphuang built after the singer's cremation in a Suphan Buri temple, etc. When these eerie stories became known, and someone claimed to win the lottery after visiting the statue, the temple became a pilgrimage site. Today, thousands rub the bark of a big tree on the grounds, looking for those magic numbers, and four more statues have been erected.

Once snubbed by the urban hip and the Thai "Hi-So," short for high society, the music found new fans in the expanding middle class, especially among white-collar workers and trend-conscious teenagers. Bangkok schools formed *luuk thung* clubs, presenting regular concerts; Rangsit University even produced an album of anguished songs about campus life. At the same time, leaders of the two most popular "Songs for Life" bands of the 1970s performed together with the Bangkok Symphony Orchestra and new clubs opened in Bangkok and elsewhere featuring groups led by similarly inclined activists. This continues today.

Many of the new singers, such as Apaporn Naskornsawan, Chakrapan (Got) Jakraphand, Dao Mayuree, Suda Srillamduan, Nujaree Sri Racha, and Yui Yartyeoh, became teen idols. Today's stars even include a blue-eyed Norwegian social worker-turned-singer, Jonas (pronounced Jonat, as Thais have trouble with "s")

Anderson, and the Dutch-British daughter of religious social workers, Christy (Krit-tee) Gibson, who have learned to enunciate the lyrics properly, and also to howl from the lungs and duplicate the severe vibrato that help telegraph the music's emotion. Such techniques come naturally to Thai vocalists, and Anderson admits he has to learn the songs note for note.

With all this new popularity and social acceptance, the number of country music companies has grown ten-fold and there now are more than a hundred vocalists with recordings, triple the figure in 1996. Where once *luuk thung* singers didn't need to be physically attractive and success relied solely on vocal prowess, now young, good-looking stars predominate, several of them making feature films along with music videos that get regular exposure on Thai language television stations. For some performers, tee-shirts have been replaced by flashy costumes reminiscent of traditional Thai dress. The line-up of eight or more dancers—key to any *luk thung* performance—is now choreographed and singers are taught by their record companies how to project more appealing personalities. An increasing number have their own web pages. And although they haven't been particularly successful, Sony, Universal, Warner, EMI and other international companies have set up Thai music divisions. So far, none of this music has been exported.

Nor is there much money to be made at home, at least not by western standards. A popular *luuk thung* singer may be paid as much as US$500-1,000 per concert, not bad considering the country's average annual per capita income is under $3,000. Most fees are much smaller, however, and personal appearances often generate more income than record sales, in part because of the widespread counterfeiting; the leading label, Grammy, in early 2002 reduced its CD price by half in an effort to compete with the bootleggers.

Where once a patronage system in the *luuk thung* business saw famous singers with up to a hundred dancers, musicians, comedians and other less famous singers on their payrolls, and the star vocalist owned everything from the dancers' dresses to the instruments, now most performers work alone, managed by their record labels or independent production companies.

Only a few of today's *luuk thung* singers have their own bands. Most travel a circuit alone, at its basic level appearing in several venues in a single night, backed by each club's house band, performing familiar songs that everyone can sing. Many of the older vocalists work for tips from the audience, earning $100 or more a night.

Bangkok's Tawan Isan Daeng is typical club. It's a huge, dark warehouse of a room that serves a menu of Isan dishes and is popular with families as well as with young men and women lonesome for Isan and looking for a cheap night out.

After nine, when a seven-piece band appears, accompanied by a lineup of dancers in matching outfits and a round-robin procession of vocalists, the small dance floor in front of the stage fills with the middle-aged and young alike, repeating the easy, gliding steps and the sinuous waggling of arms and wrists held above their heads that characterizes simple Isan dance, backed by the drone and thump and lyric message that, for an evening, takes them home.

Greasing the Reels

Foreign film companies looooooooove Thailand.

After dozens of foreign productions—from *The Ugly American*, casting Kukrit Pramoj as a fictional prime minister opposite Marlon Brando, and the early James Bond extravaganza with Roger Moore, *Man With the Golden Gun*, which turned an island in Phang Nga Bay into a tourist attraction; to most of the Vietnam war films and no-brainers by Steven Seagal and Jean-Claude Van Dame—Thailand has cultivated a behind-the-camera labor force comfortable working with foreigners, and it has become recognized as a location of choice for filmmakers at affordable rates.

It has mountains and jungles, tropical island beaches, rivers and canals, ancient ruins and villages little changed since the Stone Age. It has vintage aircraft and tanks and elephants, all in working order. It has five-star hotels, where cinema egos can get the room service they believe they deserve.

That isn't all. Thailand also has a reputation for cooperation. Virtually anything you want, if you are willing to pay for it, can be had. Want to close down traffic on one of the major roadways in Bangkok (as was done for Oliver Stone and others)? No problem. Want to halt shipping on the Chao Phraya River so you can blow up and sink a boat (as was done for Van Damme, an effort that required permission from police on both sides of the river and the marine police)? Easy as pie. Need an army of men with weapons or a fleet of helicopters? Say where and when you want delivery. Did one of the stars or production principals get thrown into jail, and you want him released? Piece of cake. Did someone die on the set and you want it to go unreported? Have a second piece of cake.

Filming is big business in Thailand, if not for the home-grown productions—whose budgets still rarely go over the US$1 million mark—then for those imported from Hong Kong, Japan, Germany, the U.K. and, most profitably, the U.S. Most of the Indochinese war films made in the past twenty years—*The Deer Hunter, Air America, Good Morning Vietnam!, Platoon, Heaven and Earth, Uncommon Valour, Casualties of War* and *Operation Dumbo Drop* among them—were filmed in Thailand.

So were Van Damme's earlier *Kickboxer* and *Street Fighter* and his more recent *Quest; Cutthroat Island,* in which the Krabi coastline masqueraded unconvincingly as the Caribbean; *The Phantom,* based on the American comic strip; *Mortal Kombat* (both of them), *The Young Indiana Jones Chronicles;* a remake of *Around the World in 80 Days,* Angelina Jolie's *Beyond Borders;* Oliver Stone's *Alexander; Bridget Jones: The Edge of Reason,* John Carpenter's *Vampires 3;* another James Bond film, this one starring Pierce Brosnan, *Tomorrow Never Dies;* Steven Seagal's *Belly of the Beast;* and, believe it or not, something called *Surf Ninjas* of the *South China Seas.*

Plus there has been a regular stream of documentaries, music videos and commercials. No one knows exactly how much this is worth to the Thai economy, although official revenues by 2003 from foreign productions had tripled since 1998, when the take was US$10 million. This is miniscule compared to the $10 billion spent by foreign visitors, but add the exposure that Thailand's sights and scenery get, presumably easing the job of the state Tourism Authority, and add to that all the unreported exchange that takes place under the table.

"You know what it cost to lease the choppers and planes for *Air America*?" a Hollywood production manager said, insisting on anonymity because he wanted to work in Thailand again.

"We're talking hundreds of thousands of dollars, all of it going straight into Air Force pockets. There were these aircraft that were supposed to be self-starting, but the batteries were dead, so we had to pay a fortune to fly in a battery starter from Lopburi. Back in the States, I could've bought an entire airplane for the same price.

"It doesn't matter," he continued, laughing, "because if the script is set in the tropics, this is the place. *Apocalypse Now* was shot in the Philippines and *The Bridge on the River Kwai* in Sri Lanka and not even tourists go to those places these days. Vietnam? Forget it. The communists didn't invent red tape, but they perfected it."

"Yes, it's a racket," said another longtime film worker, this one a resident of Thailand. "A production guy comes here with a local budget and Thailand says, 'Hey, that sounds do-able,' then a hundred actors and key crew check into hotels in Phuket, production begins, and about a week later, even the price of paint doubles or triples. What's the studio going to do? Go home? There's too much invested to do that. Of course, everybody knows this by now—when you go to Thailand, they take you for a ride. The bottom line is that it's *still* cheaper here than other places. And more professional. And when the cameras are turned off, more fun."

"You must, let me repeat that, *must* have an agent working for you in the country before you get here," said Mona Nahm, originally from Germany and a co-production coordinator for Kantana Productions, a Bangkok-based company with nearly fifty years of film and television experience. "If you come here and don't have an agent, you're going to die because the paperwork is a killer."

Mona said that when the film company for *Bloodsport*, a low-budget martial arts movie starring then-unknown Jean-Claude Van Damme, came to Thailand in 1984, the producer hadn't done his homework. When the film's point man arrived at the Bangkok airport, they had tourist visas. That stopped them until they got non-immigrant visas, which would allow them to apply for work permits and go into production. When they returned with all of their cameras and other equipment and declared its value at US$1million, they were asked to deposit a cash bond in the same amount to guarantee they would not sell it. The deposit was refundable, but the company didn't have the money, so *Bloodsport* was not made in Thailand.

"There are two categories of foreign film made in Thailand," said Skip Heinecke, a twenty-year veteran of the Hollywood PR wars, then a vice president of Royal Garden Resorts in Bangkok. "There are the ones using Thailand as a setting for somewhere else, the Vietnam films and so on, and the ones *about* Thailand. There aren't very many of the latter."

One reason was the Film Board, a section of the Prime Minister's office, created partly in response to the Japanese porn movies that were filmed in Thailand some years ago. This was a panel of forty men and women from numerous other ministries and departments that wanted to know, in the words of one production chief, "everything including the color of the leading lady's knickers." That wasn't precisely true, of course, but control was fairly strictly maintained. The application for filming in Thailand required a detailed plot synopsis along with forty copies of the script in Thai and a promise that "the filming process and end product shall not adversely affect the national security, public order or good morals."

It was the Film Board's job to see that the country was not slandered. When part of *The Deer Hunter* was shot in Patpong, for example, the scene was allowed because the movie was set in Vietnam and the sign erected outside the bar, during filming, was in Vietnamese. If the movie was about Thailand, such bars and prostitution were taboo subjects, as was Buddhism, sexually transmitted diseases (especially AIDS), drugs, and anything that might in any way denigrate royalty. This last situation resulted in moving production of the big budget *Anna and the King* (starring Jodie Foster and Chow Yun-Fat) in 1999 from Thailand to Malaysia after the Film Board rejected the first three submitted scripts for reported inaccuracies.

"And to make sure you don't submit one script and then try to film another, there're always at least two members of the Film Board present during shooting and they must sign off on all raw film before it can leave the country for processing," said Supaporn (Penny) Kanjanapinchote, who worked for twenty-three years for a Hong Kong-based film company and had a firm of her own in Bangkok. In addition, she said, Film Board representatives must be paid at least a thousand baht a day and given transportation and accommodation allowances at the same rate as that of the film crew.

The person regarded as the king of Thailand's cinema hill was Santa Pestonji, a cigar-smoking wine connoisseur whose father was a noted Thai filmmaker. Ethnically Parsi but a Thai citizen, his first big assignment was *The Killing Fields* in 1984 and he coordinated in-country services for a majority of the big-budget foreign films since. Khun Sant, as he was called, coordinated everything from transportation to hotel rooms to catering and permits to equipment to locations and sets.

He also assisted with crises, including the wildcat strike that halted filming of *The Killing Fields* in Phuket when the American studio gave private rooms to American technicians and put their local peers two to a room, tantrums Danny Glover threw during the shooting of *Operation Dumbo Drop* when he was called Khun Danny—because the honorific Thai "*khun*" sounds like the American epithet "coon," the high profile scuffle on the set of *The Beach* when local activists accused him of siding with foreigners even as they were ravaging the pristine Krabi beach, and the suicide of an assistant director during the filming of *The Phantom* in Krabi. For smaller problems, such as obtaining last-minute permission to use someone's front garden or block traffic in a neighborhood or anything else causing inconvenience, he carried an attaché case full of cash.

Smaller fish swimming in the cinema sea were the specialists, or subcontractors. One, Oy Pachara, was a production assistant who took foreign passports to the Immigration Department so all the foreigners who planned to remain in Thailand for longer than fifteen days could work legally. She said that for *Cutthroat Island* she processed two-hundred passports.

Another specialist, Jack Shirley, a CIA agent who helped organize the Thai border police's air force in the 1960s and later played a major role with Air America in the secret war in Laos, now was paid to coordinate police permits, a seemingly effortless task that he performed on his mobile phone, calling all his old cop buddies from his regular seat at the end of the Madrid Bar in Patpong. It was Jack who coordinated the sinking of the ship in the Chao Phrya River for Jean-Claude Van Damme. A big budget French film in 2002 required the closure of thirty-two public roads.

A third specialist was Richard Lair, a longtime resident of Thailand called "Professor Elephant" for his pachyderm expertise. He was hired by the Disney studio for *Operation Dumbo Drop*, a feature based on the true story of the U.S. military's moving an elephant several hundred kilometers during the war in Vietnam to replace one accidentally killed in a village, eventually dropping it from a helicopter by parachute.

Richard, who said that it made sense for the animal to be brought to Thailand from the U.S. because it was better trained than any local ones, auditioned more than a hundred elephants before he found the one he liked for other stunts, and then he worked with the *mahouts* throughout the filming, using his Thai fluency to assist in communication between Thais and the foreign crew.

One more specialist was Neville Melluish, a pin-striped insurance broker whose Bangkok office is festooned with Japanese samurai swords, machine guns, and a World War II-era bazooka, souvenirs from earlier productions. He said that for *The Killing Fields*, helicopters were leased from the Royal Thai Army and two of them crashed. They were twenty-two-year-old Hueys, noisy workhorses left over from Vietnam's war with America, he said, and not worth much. Still, when the next foreign film company came to Thailand and wanted choppers, the military said no.

"So I found an insurance company that would, for a price, insure the aircraft for more than their true value," he said, "and

I was able to guarantee the army that if one of their choppers went down, it would be replaced by a brand new one. That was for *Casualties of War*. Happily, none of them crashed."

Steve Rosse, a set decorator in the U.S. before he became a columnist for *The Nation*, a daily English language newspaper in Bangkok, worked on Oliver Stone's *Heaven and Earth*, filmed mostly in Phuket. "Oliver wanted white egrets in the rice fields," he recalled, "and we don't have white egrets in southern Thailand, so he sent a guy to Isan, who captured a couple of dozen of the birds and brought them in cages on a flatbed truck. By the time they arrived, a third were dead, another third had had their feathers blown off, and the survivors, who appeared in a long shot, little white dots in a field of green, for about two seconds, within three days were eaten by wild dogs and ferrets."

Another story was told about *The Deer Hunter*. When the studio advance man checked into the Oriental Hotel in 1978, he met a man who insisted he was a colonel in both the Thai police and the Thai army who promised to arrange all security. The "colonel" walked away with a small fortune in cash and was never seen again. It also cost the producer of another major film a substantial sum to be released from jail after he openly smoked a "Hollywood cigarette" in a popular Bangkok restaurant.

Indeed, many of Hollywood's losses are self-inflicted. "This is not a big surprise," said one production executive. "Let's admit it, Hollywood is just another word for waste. Between the big spenders—egos on an expense account—and the creative accountants, you say the word 'Hollywood' and it's an invitation to larceny."

Nor is it merely a case of the Thais getting fat from Hollywood's lavish spending. In typical Asian style, Thais also skim the earnings of other Thais. "A typical stunt," said one Bangkok-based facilitator, "is for the Thai hired to contract a crew of drivers to ask for five hundred baht a day for each one, then pay the drivers two hundred, keeping the rest for himself, and if the driver complains, fire him." Similarly, a local production secretary said she routinely kicked back twenty five percent of her salary to her boss. "So what," she said. "I still get four times what I can make in a regular job."

"And," said Skip Heinecke, "she still costs less than someone working in the same capacity in Hollywood. That's why there are so many runaway productions. In Thailand, the below-the-line crew will work long hours, seven days a week, without overtime, without complaint."

"You know about 'tea money.' This is called 'facili-tea money,'" said Supaporn Kanjanapinchote. "If you have a big budget, I can deliver. If you have a small budget, I can still deliver, but it's different. Cheaper hotels. Not so many stunts. You get what you pay for."

"The bottom line is getting the job done," said Richard Lair. "Hollywood is willing to pay fifty percent more if they know that they'll get delivery. That's what Khun Sant does. He guarantees delivery. This is true in any business, if you're going to be successful—get the job done. No matter what it costs, so long as you think you can still make a profit. And in the movie business, profit is always a hopeful guess."

"With the competition of Hollywood's so-called blockbusters in the movie houses, the audience for local films has shrunk, so not many are made these days, and the local budgets are shrinking, too," said Stirling Silliphant, Oscar-winning writer of *In the Heat of the Night*, who lived the last seven years of his life in Bangkok.

"Some of us tried to get Hollywood and New York to put money into local production of films for television, a TV series, something that would be true to Thai ways, yet commercially attractive in foreign markets. It hasn't happened yet. So for now, the talented local professionals will have to get by on what Hollywood brings. It's a good living for most of these people and let's be honest, we're all in this for the money. The glamor, too, but mostly it's the cash."

Going Troppo

Sleeping With Conrad

Somerset Maugham was delirious. Crazed by the splendor of Bangkok one day, and by the anopheles mosquito the next. He was so sick with malaria when he arrived at the Oriental Hotel, in 1923, following an arduous trek through the jungles of what was then called Burma and Siam, that when his fever rose to 103 degrees Fahrenheit (39.5 Celsius), the hotel's German manageress was overheard telling the doctor on the verandah outside his room, "I can't have him die here, you know."

Maugham didn't die in Thailand, of course (but in France, some forty-two years later), leaving instead a mark on the country's travel-cum-literary legacy. This is not unusual. Writers tend to leave their footprints in places foreign to their origin or nationality. Can anyone think of Ernest Hemingway and not think of Paris, Key West, Spain, and Africa? Are not the same associations made between Pearl Buck and China, Herman Melville and the South Seas, Jack London and the Arctic, and James Michener and a dozen very fat books whose titles were taken straight from a map? And so it has been for Bangkok, a port of call for writers for more than a century.

Joseph Conrad was a young ship's officer staying at the Sailors' Home in Singapore in 1888 when he was given command of the barque *Otago*, then tied up in Bangkok, after the captain died at sea. When Conrad reached the Siamese capital, he reported in a letter to the ship owners in Australia that the crew "suffered severely whilst in Bangkok from tropical diseases, including fever, dysentery and cholera."

At the time, the "Old Oriental Hotel" was a one-story building raised on piles offering "Family Accommodations - American Bar - Billiard Saloon - Newspapers Kept - Boats for Hire - Table *d'hote* with breakfast at 9:10 a.m., tiffin at one p.m. and dinner at seven p.m." Such luxury was unexpected and worrying to the future novelist, but he was reassured by Captain H.N. Andersen, the former sailor who owned the hotel and was reconstructing the building which survives today as the facade of the Authors' Wing, overlooking the garden and the river. The hotel admits Conrad never actually spent a night as a guest, but insists "he was a frequent patron of the hotel's facilities."

Thus, Conrad and Maugham, along with two other illustrious former guests, Noel Coward and James Michener, today have the hotel's most expensive suites named for them, each containing a number of their books and period photographs.

I've never understood the appeal of sleeping in a room where someone famous once spent the night, but it seems a popular practice in the overnight accommodation business. So many bed-and-breakfast places dating to the 1700s in the United States boast that "Washington Slept Here,"—it's become something of a joke, and the financial advantage President Clinton found in offering wealthy contributors the use of the Lincoln Bedroom in the White House is somewhat shamefully well known. Similarly, the Grand Hotel Oloffson in Port Au Prince, Haiti's most famous hostelry, has suites named for Graham Greene, Sir John Gielgud, Marlon Brando and Mick Jagger. Presumably it's a commercial scheme employed in other parts of the world as well. I digress.

Maugham's long journey from London by sea to Rangoon, then up the Irrawaddy River by steamer and overland by train, car and pony through Burma's Shan states, and on to Siam, traveling to Bangkok by train, was undertaken to produce his only real travel book, *The Gentleman in the Parlour*. (It was less than a great success when it was published in 1930 and unavailable for many years before being reprinted in 1995.) At the time of his visit, Maugham was famous as a dramatist who once had four plays running simultaneously on the London stage and as the author of several best-selling novels, including his quasi-autobiographical *Of Human Bondage* and *The Moon and Sixpence*, the latter based on the life of painter Paul Gauguin.

From his remarks about Thailand, it is clear that however willing Maugham may have been to travel rough in Burma and in the Siamese north, when his train reached Ayutthaya, he'd had enough and intended to remain aboard, saying that "if a man of science can reconstruct a prehistoric animal from its thigh bone why cannot a writer get as many emotions as he wants from a railway station?" His guide had other plans and dragged him from monument to monument, allowing him the contentment of one night on a houseboat, then led him finally to Bangkok, where in an act that proves some things never change, he was handed a card by a street tout that read: "Oh, gentleman, sir, Miss Pretty Girl welcome you Sultan Turkish bath, gentle, polite, massage, put you in dreamland with perfume soap. Latest gramophone music. Oh, such service. You come now! Miss Pretty Girl want you, massage you from tippy-toe to head-top, nice, clean, to enter Gates of Heaven."

Finally, he stumbled into the lobby of the Oriental, burning with fever that may be blamed for the erratic nature of his observations, leading him to remark on the "dust and heat and noise and whiteness and more dust" and calling Chinatown "dark, shaded, and squalid" one day and on the next being bedazzled by the city's *wats*.

"They are unlike anything in the world, so that you are taken aback, and you cannot fit them into the scheme of the things you know. It makes you laugh with delight to think that anything so fantastic could exist on this somber earth. They are gorgeous; they glitter with gold and whitewash, yet are not garish; against that vivid sky, in that dazzling sunlight, they hold their own, defying the brilliancy of nature and supplementing it with the ingenuity and the playful boldness of man. The artists who developed them step by step from the buildings of the ancient

Khmer had the courage to pursue their fantasy to the limit; I fancy that art meant little to them, they desired to express a symbol; they knew no reticence, they cared nothing for good taste; and if they achieved art it is as men achieve happiness, not by pursuing it, but by doing with all their heart whatever in the day's work needs doing."

Especially impressed by Wat Suthat, he further wrote, "With the evening, when the blue sky turns pink, the roof, the tall steep roof with its projecting eaves, gains all kinds of opalescent hues so that you can no longer believe it was made by human craftsmen, for it seems to be made of passing fancies and memories and fond hopes."

Other writers who have visited Bangkok may be too numerous to name, although the Oriental has memorialized a wide variety, including, besides the four for whom the suites were named, John LeCarre, Graham Greene, Gore Vidal, Norman Mailer, Barbara Cartland, Kukrit Pramoj—Thailand's best-known author, as well as a favorite prime minister—Alec Waugh, Romain Gary and Wilber Smith. Why did these authors get some of the most expensive rooms named after them? Some came as keynote speakers for the annual SEA Write awards, presented as an encouragement to young writers from each of the ASEAN countries and co-sponsored by the hotel.

Others were actually working. Graham Greene wrote numerous novels placed in the region—his most famous, *The Quiet American*, is centered in Vietnam—and actually wrote a letter following one of his visits (framed and hanging in the suite), calling the hotel a place where "almost anything may happen and one may meet almost anybody, from a mere author to an international crook on his way elsewhere." While Barbara Cartland—whose suite is pink, her favorite color—began writing a novel based in Thailand at the turn of the new century, a romance, *Journey to a Star*.

As vastly different as the writers were, the hotel was a part of their Thailand experience. Over the years, Maugham enjoyed telling how he almost got kicked out of the Oriental and when he returned to Bangkok many years later, perhaps remembering that early visit, he elected to stay somewhere else.

The Backpackers

Backpackers are the low-riders of tourism: youthful pilgrims in search of themselves under the guise of seeking experience and enlightenment (but for many, in fact, just getting out of the house and school), the holiday-on-the-cheap hordes who've been there and done that twice and along the way made Bangkok's Khao San Road infamous, while throwing enough money at Tony and Maureen Wheeler to allow them to fly Business Class for the rest of their lives (they own the *Lonely Planet* publishing empire).

In the 1960s, the "straight" world called such people "hippies." But backpackers are a different breed. They've partied in Goa and spent a week in an ashram and they wear the same parachute pants from Kathmandu and even take some of the same drugs, but the tie-dyed, long-haired swarm of the 1960s and early 1970s actually stood for something, or tried to, while their clones-gone-astray in the 1990s, as ubiquitous as self-indulgence and sloth, may be rebels without a cause save hanging out (or merely "hanging," as the current vernacular has it).

The differences between the generations may be understood by comparing books written about them. The first was Jack Kerouac's *On the Road*, a novel deemed unpublishable when the author's agent sent it around in the 1950s, a manic word-grenade typed in a single burst on a single roll of teletype paper, whose hero was Dean Moriarty (based on the real-life Neal Cassidy), a "sideburned hero of the snowy west" whose energy gave Keouac's creation a rush like amphetamine. He was one of Kerouac's "mad ones, the ones who are mad to live, mad to talk, mad to be saved, desirous of everything at the same time, the ones who never yawn or say a commonplace thing, but burn, burn, burn like fabulous yellow roman candles exploding like spiders across the stars and in the middle you see the blue centerlight pop and everybody goes 'Awww!'" Thus, the Beat Generation was defined; the "Beat" stood for beatitude, by the way.

Arguably, Kerouac was the father of the hippies—*On the Road* was the book that Jim Morrison and Janis Joplin and many others claimed most influential—and so it was no surprise when the same Neal Cassidy reappeared in 1964 as the driver of the painted bus that carried a group of novelist Ken Kesey's friends the Merry Pranksters from California to the New York World's Fair. The bus was called Intrepid and on the front there was a sign that warned three thousand miles of small towns, "We Have Come for Your Daughters!" In the refrigerator was a pitcher of LSD-spiked lemonade. The journey was documented in Tom Wolfe's 1968 account, *The Electric Kool-Aid Acid Test*, setting the tone for much of what followed throughout the western world.

In the 1970s, the hippies disappeared, at least in the media, elbowed aside by *Saturday Night Fever* and the Me Generation and then the Babyboomers, enfatuated first with raising their consciousness (becoming by their own boast "estholes") and then with making a million bucks buying and selling futures and bonds, and blowing it all on cocaine. No wonder that Quaalude, a horse tranquilizer that tended to make you fall down, was another drug of choice.

In the 1980s came the X Generation and Heavy Metal and Techno and Rap, and the drugs of choice now were manifestations of cocaine in its vilest forms: ice and crack. And to come down, a taste of heroin.

Meanwhile, backpackers spread like crab grass. The old hippie trail to India, Nepal and Tibet was revived, providing new blood for the communes and beach parties along the way; orgies in Goa followed by a month cleaning up in a meditation class in Varanasi.

And then they discovered Thailand, led by the nose by the Wheelers, whose second book was a patchwork guide to Southeast Asia on the cheap. Finally, in 1996, the backpackers' bible—their answer to *On the Road*—was published. This was *The Beach*, a first novel by British writer Alex Garland. As I write this, I'm looking at the back cover copy of the paperback edition: "Bangkok—the first stop on the backpacker trail. On Richard's first night in a hostel a mysterious traveler slits his own wrists, leaving Richard a map to 'the Beach.' The Beach is a legend among young travelers in Thailand: a secret island Paradise where a select community lives in blissful isolation..."

It sounded like the hippies all over again, with the comforts that a quarter century brings. On the first page of his book, Garland called Khao San Road "backpacker land. Almost all the buildings had been converted into guest-houses"—he wrote—"there were long distance telephone booths with air-con, the cafes showed brand-new Hollywood films on video, and you couldn't walk ten feet without passing a bootleg-tape stall. The main function of the street was a decompression chamber for those about to leave or enter Thailand, a halfway house between East and West."

Garland and his novel and the inevitable movie released in 2000—starring Leonardo DiCaprio, a yuppie wannabe pretending to be a backpacker; at first I thought the casting was wrong, but then I realized it was bang-on—did for the backpackers what the previous texts did for the beatniks and the hippies. Made them cliches in their own time. Except, this time around there was no substance to subvert.

Where the beats and their long-haired spawn staged a siege on society's constraints, rebelling against conformity, protesting against Vietnam and for marijuana, against Lyndon Johnson and for dancing, against hypocrisy and for ecstasy (the emotion, not the drug), against police and for sex, expanding on the vocabulary of exploration, actually trying to put their heads (as they said) into a different space, the only questions backpackers seemed to ask concerned cheap train tickets and where they could find the best banana pancakes.

These cultural flotsam and jetsam are found in greatest number in Thailand not just in the three-dollar-a-night guest houses in Bangkok's Banglampoo district (of which Khao San Road is the main drag), but during the full moon of every month in communion with their peers in ecstasy (the drug, not the emotion) on a beach on an island named Koh Pha-ngan, where, following directions found on the Internet, on the full moon of every month, an estimated eight thousand to ten thousand backpackers worship Dionysus, the ancient Greek god of partying.

(In fact, when someone pointed out that days when the moon is full are religious holidays for those who bow to the lunar calendar, the party was moved ahead one night.)

The old fishing huts on Pha-ngan are gone now, replaced by small cabins and rooms and restaurants that sell fried rice and burgers. Internet cafes, without which no backpacker could survive, sit next to shops selling black-light posters of psychedelic mushrooms and body-piercing parlors with photos on display showing all the intimate places a stud or ring can be affixed. (Bring your own anesthetic.)

Beachside bars crank up the volume and the resonant bass of techno muscles in on the natural rhythms of the heart, as the chemicals ingested go zooming to the brain, abetted by unlimited quantities of alcohol and caffeine-rich drinks called Red Bull and Caribao, the latter named for a popular local rock band. By midnight, the surf has become a toilet for partygoers disinclined to line up for the club lavatories or pay twenty-five cents for the private, beachside stalls. By two o'clock, most are drunk or stoned and those still on their feet are dancing in the sand. The last body is usually dragged away to one of the small clinics by noon.

Back in Bangkok, the veterans compare notes with new arrivals. "What was it like?" "I don't remember, mate." "Oh, man, that sounds way cool! What's the best way to get there— train or bus?"

It wasn't planned this way. *Time* magazine opined that when backpackers first hit the road in the 1970s, they were seen as "an antidote to sterile package tours, a return to travel as exploration and adventure," where anyone could be Marco Polo, travel close to the ground and get to know the "locals" and their divergent cultures. Rather than give their money to international hotel chains, they'd give their money directly to guest house owners, mom-and-pop restaurants, and street vendors. As tourists, they insisted, they were "green."

There was some truth to that. Contrast the average backpacker who remained in Thailand for the full month allowed on his or her entrance visa with the wealthy tourist who stayed at an international hotel.

This hippie redux dream was dashed quickly. Backpackers traveled like migrating herds on a predictable path, connecting beaches in India (Goa), the Philippines (Boracay), Bali (Kuta) and southern Thailand, and as true environmentalists discovered, the herds inevitably trampled the landscape flat. "They tend to be like sheep, all going to the same places," Tony Wheeler told Time. "That is a negative."

Bangkok Heart Attack

When I told my kids back in the United States that I'd decided to have open heart surgery in Bangkok, they thought I needed my head examined. Was I crazy?

I assured them I was not, said they had to trust their dear old dad, even if he was falling apart. I said my Thai cardiothoracic surgeon was London-trained and had participated in over a thousand such operations, while the cardiologist who'd been supervising my coronary health the past year, was schooled in the U.S. and practiced there for twenty years before returning to Thailand, and that Bumrungrad Hospital probably was the best in the region, including those in Singapore.

Coincidentally, I'd interviewed the CEO of Bumrungrad recently for a story about Bangkok's emergence as an Asian health care center, and was impressed even more than I'd been during my six years of residence—during which time I'd visited the hospital's dermatology, EENT and internal medicine departments, where I always got excellent care. I also talked with the resident doc at the U.S. Embassy, who told me he could send expat heart patients home and used Bumrungrad instead.

Before getting on with what happened to me in surgery, here is a part of the story I wrote following that interview with the CEO and sent to my kids, making it clearer (I hoped) why they were concerned and perhaps why they didn't have to be.

• • •

Countries are a bit like entertainers: they want to be the center of attraction and make a nice living by being so. They also want to be taken seriously. Certainly this is true in Southeast Asia, where nations compete eagerly to be a regional center for this or that, or in the current business parlance, a "hub."

Thus, Hong Kong and Singapore battle it out for pre-eminence as financial centers and telecommunications and import-export hubs, while Shanghai threatens to overtake Hong Kong by merging its stock exchange with that of Shenzhen. At the same time, Hong Kong, Singapore, and Bangkok are in a three-way contest as transportation links, and Kuala Lumpur has staked a claim as THE software manufacturing center to be reckoned with...as Myanmar and Cambodia haggle over which produces the most and best quality gems, and Thailand, Indonesia, and the Philippines all say they have the best beaches. We won't even touch the subject of where the best shopping is, nor where the most beautiful women reside.

As the members of ASEAN, and southern China (arguably a part of Southeast Asia, at least economically and culturally), scramble for control of various markets, some of them make an occasional, amusing stretch. When the Love Bug devastated computers around the world in 2001 and the culprit or culprits were said to be young hackers in Manila, for instance, then President Joseph Estrada, a onetime film actor, said his country should strive to become a center for developing anti-virus software. It sounded like a bad movie plot.

So, too, did a plastic surgeon's call in Thailand when he said Bangkok could become the world's center for sex-change operations. In fact, the doctor, himself one of a number of physicians active in waving his magic scalpel to turn one sex into another (mostly men into women), actually was on the right track. He was just taking too narrow a view.

Others in Thailand already had tried to promote the country as a destination for foreign retirees, without any notable success.

But one of the things offered to such retired persons did seem, by itself, reasonably exploitable—and that was the recognition given the country's new levels of medical proficiency.

Not long ago, if you needed medical assistance in Southeast Asia, conventional wisdom said the best—only!—places to go were Hong Kong and Singapore. I remember a half-dozen years ago asking Andrew Toth, the American consul in Bali, what his biggest problem was. He said it was trying to convince foreign visitors to the island that just because they were staying in a five-star hotel, they could not get five-star medical treatment.

"I told them that if they had anything more serious than a broken leg," he told me, "they should somehow get to Singapore. Because the hospitals in Bali didn't even provide medicine or food."

It was for this reason that many expatriates in Indonesia, and elsewhere in the region, had clauses in their medical insurance policies that covered "med-evac" (airlift) service to Singapore or Hong Kong.

Happily, medical treatment has improved in Indonesia and elsewhere in Southeast Asia in recent years, but it's still pretty shaky in much of the region. In most Southeast Asian countries, even the capital cities don't have much to brag about when it comes to modern medicine.

Of all the countries, Thailand may have improved the most, and there is no better place to start than in the office of Curtis Schroeder, the American CEO of Bumrungrad Hospital in Bangkok. He believes that Thailand's medical services now are as good as those offered in Singapore and that with prices one-half to one-third of those in that city-state, Singapore no longer can compete.

The shift began, he said, in 1997, when Bumrungrad opened its new building and six months later the baht was devalued. The Singapore dollar subsequently lost only a little of its value, but this led to its losing most of its Indonesian patients when the rupiah dropped to less than a third of its previous value, making Bangkok the more attractive destination for health care.

Schroeder also credited Bangkok's location, within quick and easy reach of numerous countries that don't offer much modern medical treatment—from Nepal and Bangladesh to Myanmar, Laos, Cambodia and Vietnam.

"These fundamentals are not specific to our hospital," Schroeder said, "—they apply to everyone in Bangkok." He also recognized that eight other hospitals (in Chiang Mai and Hat Yai as well as in the capitol) have been certified by the Swiss-based International Standards Organization (ISO), which evaluates and guarantees work systems but not services quality. However, so far, he said, Bumrungrad was (at the time of my interview in 2000) the only one with Hospital Accreditation (HA), the approval given by a non-governmental Bangkok organization that judges actual hospital care by American and Canadian standards.

To win this international acceptance and patient base, Bumrungrad sent marketing teams to meet doctors throughout the region, from Kunming to Jakarta to Bhutan, and opened fulltime offices in Dacca, Ho Chi Minh City and Yangon (staffed by a physician, who makes references), and representative offices in Phnom Penh, Colombo and Kathmandu. The hospital also began hosting medical teams from throughout the region and introduced a web page that attracted over three thousand hits a month.

"Our forms are now in Thai, English, Japanese and Mandarin," he went on, "and we have a staff of interpreters, including seven who speak Japanese. Many of our physicians are internationally trained. Our nurses receive cultural sensitivity training. For instance, Thai patients take the pills they're given without question, but Americans and Australians want to know what they're swallowing, so our nurses have to know. For our Muslim patients, they also know where Mecca is and prayer rugs are available.

"In addition, we've tried to create an international feel to the place. Much of the hospital signage is in English and Japanese as well as Thai. We offer vegetarian, western, Japanese and Oriental [Chinese and Thai] dishes on our menu and employ guest chefs from leading local hotels who create healthy gourmet lunches. We have Japanese and Thai restaurants in the hospital, along with a McDonald's and a Starbucks, and soon will have two Cybernet cafes for our patients."

The chain restaurants have drawn some criticism, with one Bangkok journalist writing "fill up now on fatty hamburgers downstairs and when your arteries are clogged come upstairs and we'll replace them." Schroeder shrugged and said they were a "way to create a world ambiance. Our lobby doesn't look or smell like a hospital. It's less intimidating. We believe this creates a better environment for healing."

This setting further includes fully-serviced apartments for friends and family members. When a man comes from Japan for heart surgery, say, he's admitted to the new hospital building and his family checks into the old one, converted to comfortable one- and two-bedroom flats.

What has been the result? In 1996, there were forty thousand international patients, including resident expatriates and foreign travelers and in 1999, there were 162,000, the largest number from the Japanese expat community, followed by Americans and British. This business, Shroeder said, represented thirty percent of the hospital revenue and it made Bumrungrad the "largest international health care provider in Southeast Asia."

• • •

That was the situation when I checked myself in, got my body bathed and shaved by three attractive Thai nurses (not an altogether unpleasant experience), and was wheeled into one of the operating rooms. Briefly, one of my arteries was completely blocked ("calcified" was the doctor's word) and two others were about fifty percent blocked. I had not had a heart attack, only recurring angina pain, so I was making the assault. Call it a pre-emptive strike.

The plan was to take a long piece of a vein from one of my legs and use it to make the bypasses that would skirt the blockages and return full blood flow to and from my heart. I was assured that it would be at least six weeks before I could lift a bar girl weighing more than thirty kilograms and that the pain in my chest and leg would go away much sooner. I also had to sign a form wherein I assumed full responsibility for whatever they did while I was sedated.

In the days that followed surgery, there were moments. Many of them. The worst may have been when the team of nurses in the Coronary Care Unit extracted the breathing device that had been inserted into my throat and it seemed to have got stuck on the spot where my gag reflex resides, so that I couldn't stop gagging and felt like what Richard Pryor described in his routine about Forgetting How to Breathe and I went at the sweet little caregivers as if I were Jean-Claude Van Damme. I make light of this, but my friend (now wife) Lamyai arrived in the middle of this affray and burst into tears.

There was also the wonderful experience a few days later having the catheter yanked from my penis.

Worst of all were paranoid fantasies equal to anything Stephen King had devised that accompanied the morphine painkiller that was delivered via one of my IV drips. I swear this is true: both nights that I was being eased and sedated by that scurrilous chemical concoction, I was totally convinced that one of the nurses on the midnight-to-eight shift was a serial killer out to murder foreigners. It was like a peyote trip I took in the early 1970s, when I fell into a suicidal pit; I knew, intellectually, that the depression was drug-induced, but that didn't mean the desire to kill myself wasn't real. Now I found myself confronting the nurse every time she approached my IV bottle with a syringe, inhospitably.

"What's that?" I demanded.

"Med-ih-CEEEEEN," she lilted in her adorable Thai accent.

"What KIND of medicine?"

"Pain-kee-LAH!" she replied.

You get the picture and will appreciate why I was pleased that on the third day I was given Tylenol with codeine instead.

Recovery was quick and by the fourth day I was complaining about the food (think airline economy class or primary school cafeteria) and enduring sponge baths delivered by nurses that made me feel like an old Buick under assault by towel boys in an East L.A. carwash .

On the fifth day, most of the ten IV ports, drains, catheters and assorted monitoring connections were removed and I was in a double room alone with one of my docs telling me I was an ideal patient. (Pants on fire.) Attitude was a large part of the process, he said. There were many men who came into the hospital for what is called "elective coronary artery bypass surgery" expecting to die—between one and two percent do—and they recovered much more slowly. To assist me, I was given what looked like a child's toy and asked to take breaths deep enough to raise three balls to the top of three chambers, thus re-expand my lungs. I was also given a red, heart-shaped pillow with the hospital's name on it to hug to my chest when I coughed, which felt like being stabbed the first few days but apparently was necessary to keep fluid from accumulating. I was told to carry the pillow everywhere the first two weeks. Sure.

Lamyai was with me at night and much of every day, helping me pee and turn over and sit up, massaging my back, changing my sweat-soaked PJs, sharing my morning rice soup, peeling and feeding me fruit that was brought by visitors. One night three friends from the bar where she worked arrived at two thirty a.m on their way home, giving the nurses on duty something to gossip about for days. Lamyai was actually encouraged to stay—it's the Thai way—and I couldn't have done it without her.

On the eighth day I went home, where I sat with three looping patches on my pump, a humungous bag of pills, my dry, splotched, nearly hairless skin reminding Lamyai of an ancient Chinese man she once worked for, wounded (and missing) veins, tender former IV entry ports, cramped muscles, aching joints, blisters on my feet from the crappy slippers the hospital gave me for my forced eight-hundred-meter marches up and down the hallway, occasional floating spots before my eyes, entrails still partially compacted, and a seven-day growth of hair that looked far better on George Michael's chin than on my torso, limbs, and genitalia, as I waited for the next adventure in my life.

I had a friend who e-mailed my kids every day I was in the hospital and when my daughter and I finally talked by phone, she said that when she heard I was bitching about the food, she knew I was going to be okay

I was, too. Within a short time after discharge, I was climbing the ninety steps to the Bangkok Skytrain without getting short of breath, the pain had stopped in my left arm, and the whole thing cost me only US$8,000. A friend of mine in the States had virtually identical surgery about the same time and it cost him US$55,000!

Okay. After all's said and done, the question is: would I do it all over again in Bangkok?

Yes. But only if the nurse who shaved me before surgery is in charge of the post-operative drugs.

The Visa Dash

My friend Chris Moore was bragging about how quickly he passed through immigration on one of his recent visa trips, then immediately through immigration again, to satisfy Thailand's Byzantine requirements to remain in the Kingdom legally.

Chris is a Canadian novelist living in Bangkok and like most expatriates in foreign countries he must leave the country of his chosen residence regularly to keep his visa current. Chris generally has a visa good for six months at a time, but he must leave the country during that period, even if only for long enough to get the requisite rubber stamp on his passport, proving an exit and re-entry. Chris told me he once did a turn-around in Singapore in eighteen minutes, a stunning accomplishment.

The time came for me to make a similar visa run and I decided to challenge his mark. Singapore's airport is remarkably efficient, so desiring an even playing field I made that my destination, too. Although I gave it no significance at the time, I was carrying a bag that weighed about twenty-five kilograms, following a week-long holiday on one of Thailand's southern islands.

Trouble arose even before I left Thailand, when the plane was an hour late in departing. This meant that I wouldn't have ninety minutes in which to do my immigration boogie, but only half an hour. That left me a very small window of exit and re-entry, should I not be so lucky as Chris, or as quick.

As we approached Singapore, I shared my concern with an airline flight attendant, who referred me to the purser, who told me not to worry. She promised to turn me over to the airline's ground staff on arrival, which she did, along with a Chinese Singaporean who worked in Bangkok and was making the same turn-around visa sprint.

We were met at the plane by a young man with a cellular telephone. We took off at a run, our guide shouting into his phone, and entered one of those conveyor belts called "people movers." Continuing to take long strides, we passed all others at a rapid clip. As we exited, my knees buckled as suddenly we were on unmoving carpet again. A second man, identically dressed, also carrying a mobile phone, met us at this point and we were passed to him like batons in a relay race.

"Do you have any luggage?" the man asked. My new friend said no and I said only the fifty kg bag, which by now was beginning to feel like a sack of wet sand with a handle. Why, I asked myself, did I always buy so many books and magazines when I traveled?

There followed two more knee-buckling people movers, which took us to the main body of the terminal, where our first immigration passage loomed. Because we had traveled at such unusual speed, there were no clerks in position to meet us. Our escort hustled two into place for us and, in under a minute, I was given permission to "enter and remain in Singapore for thirty days." ("Hey, guys," I said to myself, "would you believe thirty minutes?") I checked my watch, surprised to discover that only six minutes had elapsed.

Then we were on the run again, down an escalator and through the nothing-to-declare customs path. Even if I'd had anything to declare, I couldn't have found the breath to say what; by now, my one hundred kg bag was hanging by its strap from my shoulder and I was sweating like a pig and snorting, too.

"What nationality are you?" our guide asked.

"American," I gulped, sucking air. Trying to inject some humor into what was a painful experience, I added, "I learned...how to run...through airports...from O.J. Simpson."

"Who's that?" he said.

"You know, the football player," I panted. "He made television commercials for a rental car company, jumping over airport turnstiles while trying to make a flight. That was before they say he killed his wife."

"Never heard of him," the man said. I was beginning to like him more and more.

After that, it was up a long flight of stairs. By now, my shirt was sticking to my back, my socks were slipping into my shoes, and sweat was cascading into my eyes from some mysterious aquifer in my hair. My ears were still popping, too. Slow down, you blokes, I said to myself. You've got an "older" man in tow, twice your age and carrying a 150 kilogram bag, versus the combined weight of your cellular phone and your passport. Your legs are longer, too.

We finally reached the airline check-in counter, where a clerk mosied to our service, requesting fifteen Singapore dollars each, the airport exit fee. I said I only had Thai baht. The airline representative said I'd have to change the currency—he pointed to a booth fifty meters away—but fortunately my fellow traveler had enough Singapore dollars to cover me, and as our seats were being assigned and boarding passes were printed he accepted repayment in baht, thereby saving several precious minutes in our race back to the day's last Singapore-to-Bangkok flight.

Our guide remained behind us now and my friend and I were on our own as we galloped back through immigration, picking up an exit stamp. My two hundred kilogram bag was still on my left shoulder and I was mopping sweat with a large kerchief in my right hand.

Finally, we arrived at Gate 63, an immense room where hundreds of travelers with "carry-on" bags the size of small cars were standing in line to board. I looked at my watch. It seemed incredible, but from the time we exited the plane from Thailand and passed through the boarding gate heading for home again, only fourteen minutes had elapsed! Chris Moore, eat your heart out!

Upon my return, however, my friend Chris refused to concede defeat. His record stands, he claims, as it was unassisted.

Going Troppo

What follows probably won't make much sense, or seem funny, to *farangs* who haven't lived in Thailand for a while, but for those who have, the behavioral traits here listed will ring embarrassingly true. "Going troppo" (short for tropical) is the same thing as "going native" or, more rarely, "going bamboo," and in Thailand, as elsewhere, it means more than wearing a sarong and drinking the local beer.

From a variety of sources, some of them lost in the anonymity that accompanies much of that which is transmitted by e-mail through cyberspace—along with a few of my own observations—here's how you can tell when you, as a foreigner, have stayed in Thailand longer than most:

- You look four ways before crossing a one-way street
- You've bought a house for a Thai bar girl, or at least a cell phone
- You start enjoying Thai television soap operas and game shows and think you understand them (and think the acting is Oscar quality)
- You sleep on the table and eat on the floor
- You think it's normal to have a beer at nine a.m.
- You season your hamburger with *nam pla prik* and your pizza with ketchup
- You haven't had a solid stool in five years
- A Thai traffic cop waves you over for a minor infraction and you automatically reach for your wallet

- You always take something to read in the taxi, so you'll have something to do when it takes half an hour to travel less than a kilometer
- You carry an umbrella on sunny days to keep your skin white
- As a straight male, you start holding hands with your male friends in public
- You stop *wai*-ing (the prayer-like greeting gesture) beggars, waitresses, and go-go girls
- You give up deodorants and use talcum powder instead
- You tell someone the time is three o'clock when it's actually a quarter to four
- You think a calendar is more useful than a watch
- You stop thinking that a girl riding pillion on a motorbike, side-saddle, wearing a mini-skirt, with one toe pointing to the ground, while putting on make-up, is anything out of the ordinary
- You think opening a restaurant is a good idea
- You wear rubber slippers to a job interview
- You meet someone named Steve and you call him "Sa-teve"
- You realize that virtually everything you own—your wardrobe right down to your underwear, your watch, your DVDs, even your Viagra—is counterfeit
- You keep your bus fare in your ear
- You keep toilet paper on the table instead of in the toilet
- The footprints on your toilet seat are yours
- You know that the braking distance for vehicles traveling at ten kilometers an hour is two meters and that the braking distance for vehicles traveling at one hundred kilometers an hour is also two meters
- You aren't surprised when the woman next to you in the bar is eating insects
- Later that night, you kiss the woman with the beetle breath
- You believe that buying a gold chain is an acceptable courtship ritual
- You can't remember the last time you wore a tie and you think a safari jacket and jeans constitute formal wear

- You no longer trust air you cannot see, or water so clear you will swim in it
- You start drinking water from the spigot
- You can sleep standing up on the bus, Skytrain or subway
- You discover that your girlfriend is the *mia noi* of your boss
- You buy things at the start of the month and take them to the pawn shop at the end of the month
- You think motorcycles on the sidewalk and pedestrians in the street is normal
- You cover your mouth when you pick your teeth, but openly pick your nose
- You describe anyone who has ever lived within a two-kilometer radius of you as "my brother"
- You go home and wonder where all the white people came from
- You start reading comic books instead of real books
- You stand in the shadow of a telephone pole while waiting for the bus
- You understand when your Thai wife says, "My friend you" or "Same same different"
- When asked to name your favorite Thai restaurant, you say KFC
- You start to find western women attractive again
- You realize that you frankly never have a clue what's really going on
- You have a silly grin on your face

The *Farangs*

Many Thais blame the Caucasian interloper for much of what's wrong with Thailand. Unfairly, the American financier George Soros was charged with pushing Thailand's and then much of the rest of Asia's economy to its knees in 1997 when he began speculating on the value of the Thai baht. He previously had "broken" the Bank of England with his crafty foreign exchange transactions, so there was reason to suspect he'd had a similar effect on the collapsing value of the Thai currency, but to overlook other factors endemic in Thailand—such as corruption and greed—was to make Mr. Soros a convenient scapegoat.

Other critics say Thailand wouldn't have the sex industry that gives the country such an unsavory international reputation if it weren't for American military men here during the war in Vietnam—ignoring the fact that prostitution existed in Thailand for centuries before the first *farang* sailed up the Chao Phrya River, and that today the industry is controlled almost exclusively by Thais, with Thais contributing the largest customer base, virtually all of the sex workers, ownership and management of venues, as well as the cops who are responsible, for reasons of their own, for the lax enforcement of laws against the trade.

Some pundits get personal, and none more harshly than Mont Redmond, himself a *farang*, describing in his book, *Wondering into Thai Culture* (1998), the first Europeans as "big-bodied adventurers from thimble-sized countries, odd in color and custom, and unaccountably fierce or friendly at unimaginable distances from their native land...meddlesome creature(s), inclined to excess in everything but good manners and humility." His rant continued, but that's enough to give you a feel for how he felt about his fellow round-eyes. Not that his view was entirely indefensible.

Of course, there are many who praise the *farang*, if not in words then in deed, most often in the form of flattery inherent in the speed with which much of *farang* culture and conveniences have been welcomed, copied, adapted and merchandized. Many have written of the West's influence on the East and I don't think I have anything new to say, except that I find it somewhat amusing when some of the Thais who are most outspoken in criticizing *farangs* are the ones who: drive a Mercedes-Benz or a BMW; educate their kids in England, the United States or Australia; fill up their closets with Italian shirts; worship golf to the point of naming some of their children after the game; bet on European football teams; and wouldn't be caught dead drinking anything but expensive French wines and Johnny Walker Black. And you ought to see the Thai Buddhists during the Christmas season; I thought Americans knew how to shop!

There's nothing new about this. The first Thai head of state to travel outside the region, Rama V (Chulalongkorn) visited Europe in 1897 and returned wearing a top hat and tails. He brought back Waterford crystal from Ireland, Severes porcelain and Baccarat goblets from France, Italian Murano glass, Royal Crown Derby plates from England, and introduced Western architecture to Thailand.

Which is not to be construed as negative comment on my part, so long as the preference for Western things and ways is genuine and unaccompanied by slurs against their origins. Like many *farangs* living in the Thailand, I've crossed over, too. I have a Thai family and a house upcountry, most of my diet is Thai (even including insects), I drink Chang beer and have a respectable library of books about Thailand, assembled in a so-far futile attempt to understand the country and culture that I choose to call mine for however long the Department of Immigration renews my annual visa.

I'm also trying to understand my peers and have pushed them into what I hope will become, for the reader, helpful groups:

1. **Tourists** from Europe, the Americas and what the TAT calls "Oceania," meaning Australia and New Zealand, comprise what probably is the most visable alliance or class, although their representation in the total visitor numbers is small. In 2001, only twenty five percent of those who presented their passports on entering the Land of Smiles were from Europe, under seven percent were from North and South America, just over four percent from Oceania. More than fifty seven percent, on the other hand, came from East Asia. Maybe all those Japanese, Taiwanese, and Koreans blended in more easily. Or, as Mont Redmond noted, they were not so tall or loud and thus not so noticeable. And probably the male of the Asian species wore slacks and a nice shirt, instead of a tank top with a lewd slogan, baggy shorts, running shoes, a base-ball cap, and a belly pack belted over a barrel of flesh. I shudder when I see such creatures. In any case, the word *farang* usually is applied only to Caucasians. In 2001, they totaled a third of the country's ten million visitors. That's about ten thousand new *farangs* a day, enough to give one pause. [See "Tourism," page 197.]

2. **Businessmen** may comprise the next largest group of *farangs* in Thailand. These are the investors and minority partners in many Thai companies that probably wouldn't exist if the foreigners didn't want to invest. Many are two-year "package" businessmen given a salary far larger than his or her Thai partner, a cushy housing allowance, a car and a driver, and private school tuition for the kids. When I moved to Thailand, my prospective landlady asked what sort of "package" I had. I said I was self-unemployed. The rent fell twenty five percent.

   Many of the package men, and their wives—who are banned from taking jobs for pay and thus turn to charita-ble work and, often, alcohol—rarely exit their Western bubble while here. Aside from the reserved and polite Thais in their offices, their only regular contact with the local population may be limited to household help, their drivers, merchants in the neighborhood, and, dare I say it, bar girls. Many marriages don't survive the stress attached to the latter.

Leisure activity frequently is planned for these *farangs*, by the American Chamber of Commerce or the more socially inclined embassies, most notably those from Australia and the U.K., and for the wives various women's clubs. Some join local rugby teams and participate in other contests where a majority are expats, too. For those from the U.K., there are plenty of Irish and British pubs. For all there are numerous jazz and blues venues. Most of their holiday hotels are run by Germans and Swiss. The hypermarkets are owned by the Europeans, too, and there are hundreds of McDonald's, 7-Elevens, Dunkin' Donuts, Starbucks, KFCs and Pizza Huts.

In Thailand, because numerous jobs are prescribed for foreigners, non-Thai lawyers, accountants, architects and other professionals work as "consultants," a line on the subsequent resume that the job-holder may have trouble explaining in the next job interview back home. No matter. When the interviewer sees the word "Bangkok," the two-year hole in the guy's career will be forgiven with a knowing wink and a question about the Thai women.

It should be noted that there also are many long-time *farang* businessmen in Thailand. These include, for example, Bill Heinecke, head of the Minor group of companies, an American who was born in Thailand (when his father headed up the Voice of America) and now is a Thai citizen; Denis Gray, who helped cover the final days of the war in Vietnam for the Associated Press and is now the bureau chief for the same wire service, a job he's held for more than thirty years; Patrick "Shrimp" Gauvain, best-known for his bar girl calendars but head of his own advertising company; Father Joe Maier, an American Catholic priest who's worked with the poor for thirty-plus years; and Tim Young, father and manager of Thailand's most popular singer, Tata Young. Most in this category have Thai families and are here for life.

3. **Embassy People** may be the hardest group to peg, because it's so diverse. Virtually every Western country has a diplomatic mission in Bangkok, more than sixty in all, from Albania to the Holy See. Given the small number of expats from some of the countries in residence in Thailand, and a limited number of visitors, many of the embassies and consular offices are quite small. Understandably, it is others, notably those of the United States, Australia and various European nations that dominate the embassy scene.

   The largest diplomatic community is the one from America. It surprises people when they're told that the Bangkok embassy is the second or third largest embassy in the world (behind Cairo and the Philippines). The embassy grounds and ambassador's compound sprawl across Wireless Road in Bangkok, covering an area almost the size of a small country, but the reason is no secret. From the time of the war in Vietnam, the Drug Enforcement Agency and other American surveillance organizations have based their operations in Bangkok, helping justify the construction of a new building in 1999 that is now a model for embassies everywhere, impregnable even to rocket attack.

   Other western embassies, notably the British, the Australian, the Dutch, the Danish, the French and the German, occupy similar compounds with fences and walls behind which gardeners tend lush gardens with canals and lakes, creating park-like retreats in one of the noisiest and ill-planned cities in Asia. Those who report for work here each day are nearly as diverse as tourists in their backgrounds, jobs, and personal pursuits, but their lives resemble the "package" businessmen. They, too, come and go, and while here they are wrapped in a legal cloak and offered the comforts and steady contact with "home," thus they also are distanced in many ways from their host country, even when it may be their job to decide whether or not Thai citizens are worthy of a visa or the subject of an investigation.

4. **Non-Government Organizations** (NGOs) are both a more diverse and a more heterogeneous group, defined by their variant do-gooder causes. One organization tries to help bar girls learn enough English to avoid being taken advantage of by their customers. Many want to save the elephant. ECPAT, the organization dedicated to End Child Pornography in Asian Tourism, has its headquarters in Bangkok, too. The United Nations has hordes of people in the same city writing reports on human rights and ways to increase rice production.

   Generally, this foreign group interacts with Thais better, or at least more consistently, than the previous three *farang* categories, and many are more strident of voice. Surely their contributions have been great, from the time of the arrival of the first Christian missionaries three hundred years ago, accelerating in an almost runaway manner since the first Peace Corps volunteers from America started showing rural farmers how to dig wells in the 1960s.

5. **Bar hounds** are the easiest to identify. They're in the same place almost every night, or in a variety of similar places, all of them serving booze and companionship at an affordable price. Sex may not be the only reason these *farangs* came to Thailand, but it surely is one of the most important ones. And it's the reason they stay, although many actually marry girls they meet in the bars and retire somewhat from the scene. A survey conducted by the Thai government in 2003 turned up fifteen hundred *farang* husbands of Thai women in the Northeast alone, among them, sadly, three of the men who were taken hostage in 2004 in Iraq and Saudi Arabia and beheaded.

Many of these men are retired, living on pensions. Others teach English, do whatever they can to earn just enough to pay at least one bar fine a week. Many are alcoholic.

6. The most intriguing *farangs* may be the **Runaways**, the bandits, social outcasts and disgruntled won't-go-home-againers who back where they came from are called "tax-dodgers" or "deadbeat dads" or, in many cases, bail-jumpers and convicted criminals. At a Fourth of July party a few years ago—one of the great annual *farang* events—I met a man who works as a fraud buster for western insurance companies, tracking down people who faked their deaths, then came to Southeast Asia to hide. And hardly a month goes by without a story in one of the newspapers about a *farang* being sent home to face an outstanding arrest warrant.

   In the same group, more or less, are the ex-spooks and Vietnam veterans who stayed. Three members of the Vietnam Helicopter Association bought a bar at Nana Plaza and the guy who was the Bangkok bureau chief of the CIA during the same conflict for many years owned a popular expat bar in Patpong. A third set himself up in Thailand with money earned smuggling people into Thailand from Laos and later nearly lost his residency when caught smuggling marijuana. Still another, the legendary Tony Poe, who trained and led the Hmong army in Laos and paid a dollar for every set of Vietnamese ears brought to him (some of which he stapled to his CIA reports), and was reputed to have been the model for Colonel Kurtz in *Apocalypse Now*, returned to the States with his hilltribe wife only because the Thai government got tired of his boozy fights.

There are other, smaller groups. *Farangs* who come to Thailand to study Buddhism (some have become monks) or massage or aromatherapy. Journalists assigned by their bosses to cover the region, who make the Foreign Correspondents Club of Thailand a frequent stop following work to sup, sip and diss the country in which they work, and tell each other how they'd run Thailand if they had the chance.

It's possible to belong to more than one group. Many of us do. I'm part journalist, part barhound (with a Thai family and house in the Northeast) and I contribute part of almost every week to Father Joe Maier's efforts in the slums.

Do we share anything in common, other than our big bodies, pale pigment and lack of manners and humility? Surely. I think most male *farangs*, visitor or resident, have at some time thought of themselves as a sort of "target," someone perceived as having money, or at least enough to share, causing some Thais to go after them like a heat-seeking missile. In his paranoia, probably rooted in reality, he also may think Thai men don't like him because of this wealth and advantage, but also because he takes so many Thai women away so easily. Many *farang* males, in turn, condemn Thai men when they hear how frequently they have deserted their wives and children, or have taken second wives.

Another shared trait is a changed, or changing, regard for the countries of our birth. Living abroad alters anyone's point of view, if only to sharpen one's previously held beliefs, and many go home with a repertoire of wonderful stories to tell, but are glad to be back where everything more or less works all the time, and life is more comfortably familiar. Others feel more estranged from the lands of their origins and complain about where they came from as much as about where they are. These are the ones who stay.

Inevitably, the latter disdain western media and the way it reports the world's news, because the coverage is so Euro-centric. Why, we wonder, do so many western countries give Asia and Asians so little regard? Living in Thailand offers an alternative take on many things and in time some of us embrace the Asian ways, rejecting at least some of the western ones.

In any case, most *farangs* tend to flock together. We wheel our psychological wagons in a circle, and hang out with other *farangs* most of the time, constantly comparing notes, praising and criticizing our hosts by turn, going home and coming back again, always shaking our heads in amazement; some are so bold as to write books. And however many conclusions we reach, in the end we likely haven't a clue.

Acknowledgments

"It's Not Whisky," "The Rubber Barons," "Sleeping with Conrad," "A Buffalo Named Toey," "Fun & Games in the Slums," and "Thailand—-Superlative!" previously appeared in *Sawasdee* magazine (Thailand).

"Greasing the Reels" appeared in *Manager* magazine (Thailand).

"The King Swings" appeared in *Asia Times* (Thailand) and *Winds* magazine (Japan).

"Venus Envy" appeared in *Metro* magazine (Thailand) and HQ magazine (Australia).

"The Country Club" appeared in *Arena* magazine (U.K.).

"The Bodysnatchers of Bangkok" appeared in *Maxim* magazine (U.K.).

"Country Music, Thai Style" appeared in *Wire* magazine (U.K.).

"Visa Dash" appeared in the *Asian Wall Street Journal* (Hong Kong).

"Thai Aphrodisiacs: Food That Makes You Strong" appeared in *Fah Thai* (Thailand).

Another version of "On the Eat-a-Bug Trail" appeared in *Ego* magazine (U.S.).

Part of "Bangkok Heart Attack" appeared on a web page published by Hakuhodo, the Japanese advertising agency.

Selected Bibliography

Bishop, Ryan and Robinson, Lillian S., *Night Market: Sexual Cultures and the Thai Economic Miracle*, Routledge (New York and London), 1998

Hollinger, Carol, *Mai Pen Rai Means Never Mind*, John Wetherhill Inc. (Tokyo), 1965; Asia Books (Bangkok), 2000.

Hoskin, John, *The Supernatural in Thai Life*, Tamarind Press (Bangkok), 1993.

Klausner, William J., *Reflections on Thai Culture*, The Siam Society (Bangkok), 1981.

McVey, Ruth, editor, *Money & Power in Provincial Thailand*, Institute of Southeast Asian Studies (Singapore) & Silkworm Books (Chiang Mai), 2000.

Moore, Christopher G., *Heart Talk*, Heaven Lake Press, (Bangkok), 1998.

Pasuk Phongpaichit and Chris Baker, *Thaksin: The Business of Politics in Thailand*, Silkworm Books (Chiang Mai), 2004.

Pasuk Phongpaichit and Sungsidh Piriyarangsan, *Corruption & Democracy in Thailand*, The Political Economy Center (Bangkok) & Silkworm Books (Chiang Mai), 1994.

Pasuk Phongpaichit and Sungsidh Piriyarangsan and Nualnoi Treerat, *Guns, Girls, Gambling, Ganja*, Silkworm Books (Chiang Mai), 1998.

Redmond, Mont, *Wondering into Thai Culture*, Redmondian Insight Enterprises Co. (Bangkok), 1998.

Wyatt, David K., *Thailand: A Short History*, Silkworm Books (Chiang Mai), 1982.